And all drank the same spiritual drink. For they drank from the spiritual Rock that followed them, and the Rock was Christ.
1 Corinthians 10:4

The Rock Speaks

Ten Lessons based on 1 Corinthians 10:4

Cindy STEINBECK

CONCORDIA PUBLISHING HOUSE • SAINT LOUIS

Published 2016 by Concordia Publishing House
3558 S. Jefferson Avenue, St. Louis, MO 63118-3968
1-800-325-3040 · www.cph.org

All photos used by permission. Thank you, Cecy Urquiza,
Bill and Regina Orr, Kathy Kelly, and Craig Olson.

Photo page 1: Running Eagle Falls in Glacier National Park,
Montana. Art/images: Shutterstock, Inc; iStockPhoto.com;
dollarphotoclub.com

Manufactured in the United States of America

1 2 3 4 5 6 7 8 9 10   25 24 23 22 21 20 19 18 17 16

Thank you, Allen, my brother and friend, for working through this manuscript with me. Thanks, Mom and Dad, for cheering me up and onward. Thank you, Ryan, Caitlin, Bradley and Amelia, Stacy and Bryan, and Cecy, for your love and friendship. Ted, thank you for sharing your vast knowledge of this amazing earth, our temporary home.

Table of Contents

The Rock Speaks!

Rocks cannot talk, but rocks speak! Rock, in its many forms— including soil, sand, stones, hills, valleys, and mountains— has spoken to me. I have collected rocks, observed grand rocks from a distance, and climbed rocks. I have held a tiny piece of rock in the palm of my hand, looking in wonder at its unique form. I have studied rocks with a magnifying glass and under a microscope. I have used rocks as tools and as decorations in my home.

The scientific study of rock—geology—can be an entire life's work. Mineralogy is only one aspect of geology. Studies within mineralogy include mineral origin and formation, classification, distribution in the world, and how civilization has used specific minerals. Breaking the discipline down further, there is physical mineralogy (that is, the physical attributes of minerals), as well as chemical mineralogy, biomineralogy, and optical mineralogy. Mineralogy is built on the principles of crystallography, the study of the crystalline forms within minerals that form the rocks. The types of studies within this field are extensive too. Some universities offer specializations in these fields, training people for careers in areas such as inorganic chemistry and physics.

Scientific study and categorization of minerals and crystals began in the fifteenth century. To date, more than 4,500 types of minerals have been categorized. Some are common, some less common, but most are rare. We recognize diamonds, silver, and gold as common minerals. Names like quartz, pyrite, and talc may be less familiar but are abundant. Minerals and crystals are made up of chemical elements as well as electrons, neutrons, and protons.

The complex study of minerals and crystals, elements and electrons, continues to unfold before the eyes of scientists. God is the creative genius, the Creator of rocks that some spend a lifetime studying.

While not visible to the unaided human eye, there is always movement in rock through molecular activity. In a fabulous parallel, God created life in such a way that even when, by outward appearances, something is perfectly still, there is movement. Also, the authors of the Scriptures were moved by rocks and often used rocks to describe the work and movement of God the Father, God the Son, and God the Holy Spirit. Rocks have moved me to action, to deeper faith and trust; rocks have moved me to cry out for help and mercy.

Rocks cannot talk, but they can speak! They say, "Pay attention to God's Word and notice how the writers used rocks to call us into deeper faith." In *The Rock Speaks,* we will study the words of the faithful, who were moved by rock in its many forms, and our faith will be challenged and moved to a deeper understanding and appreciation of how God moves for us, in us, and through us.

Soil in which food grows is the foundation for all life. Human life cannot exist apart from food in the form of fruits, vegetables, grains, and nuts that grow from soil on the land. Milk, cheese, and eggs are the products of animals that are sustained by food from the soil. Animals we eat are sustained by the soil. The fish and sea creatures we eat live in waters that are held in place by land and are sustained by an ecosystem based in the ground (or floor) of the body of water. The water we drink and use to grow food crops and process food comes from the earth.

We don't need to be agriculturalists to understand and grow as we study the words of Scripture in *The Rock Speaks*. We embrace the knowledge that we rely completely on products of the soil, even when we buy them from a grocery store. Modern society may be more removed from the soil than previous cultures, but perhaps we will come to see that differently too as our journey through *The Rock Speaks* opens our eyes to our closeness to the land. The knowledge we draw from images of various forms of rock used throughout the Scriptures will guide us as we journey to a deeper faith in the Rock, Jesus Christ.

Paul declared, "And all drank the same spiritual drink. For they drank from the spiritual Rock that followed them, and the Rock was Christ" (1 Corinthians 10:4). Paul's interpretation of the desert event, which saved the lives of the children of Israel as they wandered through the rock, is the verse that led me to write *The Rock Speaks*. Christ, The Rock, goes before and after us as well, surrounding us with His holy life.

Rock and the Church

Imagine walking across the land with Jesus, hearing Him proclaim Himself in the synagogues made of rocks and on the rocky hillsides, in the cities built from rocks and on the rocky shores of the lakes. Imagine the interactions between Jesus and His followers as they traveled the rocky paths or ducked to pass under archways in rock walls that marked the entrance into regions like Caesarea Philippi.

Matthew recorded Jesus' and Peter's interaction, which took place within a conversation about bringing bread or not bringing bread for their journey. They talked about being aware of the false teaching of the

religious leaders, which was completely contrary to Jesus' message of hope and healing. Jesus, the bread of life, reminded the disciples that He had fed five thousand, and I imagine He also reminded them of His words "I am the bread of life" (John 6:35). Jesus asked Peter, "Who do you say that I am?" and without hesitation, Peter answered, "You are the Christ, the Son of the living God" (Matthew 16:16). Jesus declared, "You are Peter, and on this rock I will build My church, and the gates of hell shall not prevail against it" (v. 18).

"This rock" upon which the Church is built is Peter's confession of Jesus' identity as the Christ, the Son of the living God. We gather in our churches to hear Christ proclaimed, to speak our confession, to remember our adoption into the family of God through Baptism, to pray, to praise, and to receive the Sacrament, the bread of life that is Christ's body and blood shed for us. We step out of the sanctuary, carrying with us our confession, "You are the Christ, the Son of the living God," with us every moment of our daily lives.

Jesus, the Word of God, proclaimed the coming of the kingdom of God through His life wherever He was. Wherever we are, we proclaim Christ. I wrote *The Rock Speaks* as my testament of faith that Jesus is the Christ, the Son of the living God. It will become clear to you, as you study God's Word in these pages, that I hear The Rock speaking His message in the Scriptures through dust and sand, stones and land, hills and mountains.

God's rich blessings in Christ as you journey into *The Rock Speaks*!

The Author

Chapter One

DUST

Dust is simply a very small particle of rock, and so with dust we begin our journey into *The Rock Speaks*. Living in the middle of a vineyard means living with constant dust. Tractors and trucks traveling the gravel road to my house cause tiny particles to fly through the air, filter through closed windows, and settle on my furniture. The same is true for my car and patio table. An hour after I dust, I see tiny particles floating in the air and settling back down.

My puppy runs through the plowed field on summer days and dust billows around her. The larger particles form her footing; the smaller particles puff up into a cloud and then fall back down. Dust settles into her coat. When I bathe her, the water turns a dusty brown, and it takes many shampoos and rinses to clean the dust from her fur. I can walk in that same plowed field, and whether I am wearing shoes or sandals, my feet are covered with dust.

Cindy and her puppy, Cri Cri, stirring up dust in the soil of the garden.

I've driven through a dust storm in New Mexico on a spring day. At times the dust was so thick, I thought I would have to pull the car over and wait for the storm to pass. Cars can be damaged by severe dust storms if the filters become clogged. Some areas of the world endure such fierce dust storms that people suffocate for lack of oxygen in the air. In those regions, literally, walls of dust blow through the sky.

One hot summer day, I was visiting with a friend near her horse barn. A very large dust devil blew through an open field toward us. I cried out, "It's heading right for us!" We ran toward a parked car but didn't have time to get inside. We hid behind the car, holding our faces in our hands, bodies hunched over as we tried to protect ourselves. The dust devil passed over the car but had also gone under it. We stood and looked at each other and burst into laughter. We were covered with dust!

Dust is an everyday occurrence, and dusting is a never-ending chore—not just in my home in the vineyard, but everywhere. The action word *dusting* gives us a clue to the unending task—*dust* plus *ing* forms its own action. When I clean dust off my hutch, I'm dusting. When I clean dirt from my kitchen floor, I'm "cleaning" or "sweeping," not "dirting." We buy dust mops and dust rags!

Dust, while certainly an annoyance, can also be a constant reminder of who we are and where we came from. Dust was created as part of the earth, and God saw that it was good. Dust is a window into our Creator, the Rock, our God. Dust also reminds us that although we might prefer to sweep it away or sweep it under the rug to ignore it, we will return to dust one day. Dust settles, but we don't and won't settle for anything less than what God intended for us to learn through the dust.

From Dust to Life

The creation account in Genesis reveals God's handiwork as He created the heavens and the earth by His Word. He spoke light and darkness and it was so; He spoke the land and seas into creation; He spoke fish and animals into being. Our all-powerful God—through the Word—spoke, and the universe, the earth, and every particle on the earth was so. The apostle John declares Christ as that Word, present in creation; John declared that Jesus, made flesh to dwell among us, was present and active, creating all that is (John 1:1–3).

The first mention of dust in the Scriptures is in Moses' account of the sixth day of creation: "Then the Lord God formed the man of dust from the ground and breathed into his nostrils the breath of life, and the man became a living creature" (Genesis 2:7). As we ponder dust and our relationship with God through the dust, it's important to reflect on the words Moses chose when writing the creation account. These are the action-packed words in this short verse connected to dust: formed, breathed, breath, life, living, and creature ("being" in the RSV and NIV).

God formed man from the dust of the ground. To form means "to bring together or combine parts, to create." The Hebrew word for form, *Yatsar*, means "to frame, to initiate and structure, to fashion." If you've ever played in dust—drawn a smiley face with your finger, for example—then you will know that human hands cannot form dust. Now consider that God formed the intricately woven human body from dust. This is impossible to comprehend! Nevertheless, we are called to faith in the handiwork of our Creator. David's words could have been Adam's words too: "I praise You, for I am fearfully and wonderfully made" (Psalm 139:14).

God breathed breath into man's nostrils. Breathing breath into dust requires blowing, pushing air out. Blowing into dust causes the particles to move away. The breath of God didn't destroy the formed dust; the breath of God brought the dust particles together and created the fully formed human body. Again, this is impossible to imagine! Yet we are called to believe, to trust, that the breath of God created life out of the dust of the ground.

God breathed the breath of life into man. These powerful words are evidence of God's intimacy with created man. God's breath is the breath of life. God created the rest of the world through His Word, but He created man by forming the dust and breathing life into it.

Life is a rich word and takes on additional meaning when we explore the Hebrew equivalent. *Chay* means "a unified whole: mind, body, and spirit." Therefore, Moses' creation account shows us that "life" doesn't narrowly mean the existence of just the body; rather, it encompasses the creation of the whole being. In Hebrew, the words "God breathed into his nostrils the breath of life" describe the God-breathed soul of man. To see

God's creation of man as only a body is to miss the totality of God's life-creating breath; life includes mind, body, spirit, heart, and soul.

Moses could have ended his sentence at "God breathed into his nostrils the breath of life," but he continued with these rich words: "and the man became a living creature [or being]." The living God created a living being through forming and breathing; God imparted life through dust and breath. The result of God's action, His forming and breathing, was a living being.

The Hebrew word *nephesh* ("being") occurs 775 times in the Old Testament. The source of the "being" of animals is the ground; the source of "being" of man is dust and the breath of God. *Nephesh* means "living being." *Nephesh*, like *chay*, implies the total self—body, mind, spirit, soul, emotions, and senses.

The limitations we face when trying to make something good out of dust remind us that our Creator is just that, *Creator*. God spoke light and darkness, sun and moon, earth and water into existence. God could have chosen to speak man into being as well. Instead, God chose intimate creation through touch to form man from the dust of the ground. God could have spoken breath into man, but instead God chose to breathe breath into man's nostrils. God chose to intimately connect man with the dust of the ground. God chose to intimately connect Himself with man through forming and breathing.

As we deal with the annoyance of dust, we are called to draw our attention to our Creator and to give thanks that He created man out of dust. But our relationship to dust doesn't end there; we must explore more to grasp God's continual work through the dust.

FROM LIFE TO DUST

God formed Adam from the dust of the ground and breathed into him the breath of life, creating a living being. The account continues: "And the LORD God planted a garden in Eden, in the east, and there He put the man whom He had formed" (Genesis 2:8). God formed; God breathed; God planted; God put. The actions of God created a human being in His image. The actions of God sustained the life of the man He created. God's actions created the gift of life.

The actions of man, as we know, created a mess.

God placed one tree in the middle of the garden and gave the command, "You may surely eat of every tree of the garden, but of the tree of the knowledge of good and evil you shall not eat, for in the day that you eat of it you shall surely die" (Genesis 2:16–17). God could have left that part out, just as He could have created Adam by a word. God chose to command—"don't"—to give Adam and Eve opportunity to obey and worship. Rather than viewing the command as opportunity to worship, Adam and Eve saw it (after Satan's deception) as a restriction they could challenge.

Adam and Eve's attempt to free themselves from a God-declared opportunity for obedience and worship led to their punishment and death. They were created to live eternally; they chose disobedience and death. God said, "By the sweat of your face you shall eat bread, till you return to the ground, for out of it you were taken; for you are dust, and to dust you shall return" (Genesis 3:19).

Adam and Eve journeyed from fullness of life in the garden that God planted to sustain life to the promise of toil for food in the soil and the promise of dying and returning to the dust. They saw their nakedness for the first time. Scripture states that before they disobeyed God, "The man and his wife were both naked and were not ashamed" (Genesis 2:25). After the fall, "the eyes of both were opened, and they knew that they were naked. And they sewed fig leaves together and made themselves loincloths" (Genesis 3:7). Humiliated and disappointed, Adam and Eve tried to hide themselves as a way of covering their failure to obey and worship.

Before disobedience, they felt no guilt, no embarrassment, and no shame. After disobedience, they felt all three. Guilt and shame are different. Highlighting the distinction will help us understand ourselves and our relationship to the dust and, more important, to the life from the dust to which God calls us.

Guilt correctly leads us, through our God-given conscience, to say, "I *have done* wrong." That confession leads to "God, I'm sorry, and I deserve punishment for what I've done." Guilt owns the wrong; guilt faces the facts; guilt receives correction and punishment.

Shame, on the other hand, comes from a position of fear and brokenness and says, "I *am* wrong!" This declaration leads to hiding, denying, blaming, covering up, and lying. Adam and Eve knew they were guilty the moment they fell to Satan's promise, "Your eyes will be opened, and you will be like God, knowing good and evil" (Genesis 3:5). They looked at each other and experienced embarrassment and vulnerability. They took immediate action to cover their private parts. Adam and Eve took further action and hid from God in shame. God found them hiding and asked, "Who told you that you were naked? Have you eaten of the tree of which I commanded you not to eat?" (Genesis 3:11).

Guilt came from Adam and Eve's new freedom as they journeyed away from God and defied His command. They disobeyed God and would be punished. Guilt alone would have offended God and would have invoked the punishment and the promise. But shame also became part of their experience of freedom. Shame created a flailing attempt to cover their wrong. From a position of shame, they hid, denied, blamed each other and the serpent for their disobedience, and tried to cover their disobedience with lies. Adam even chose to blame God: "The man said, 'The woman whom You gave to be with me, she gave me fruit of the tree, and I ate'" (Genesis 3:12).

Life now included vulnerability before each other and a desire to hide their most private parts from each other. Life also included a fear of vulnerability before God and a desire to hide from Him. They had known an intimate relationship with God and with each other. Their disobedience led to their realization that they were naked. But far more than that, their disobedience led to hiding from the reality that they set into motion the fulfillment of God's promise that if they ate from the tree, they would die and return to dust.

The first few chapters of the Bible give us much to consider about the fact that we have inherited, from Adam and Eve's original sin, their punishment: our own death and return to dust. Trying to deny our own mortality, even as we sing and declare that we are going to live in heaven with Jesus forever, is an unfortunate result of both our Christian culture and our world culture.

Here are just a few examples of hiding from our return to the dust:

- Aging is seen as unfortunate; general appeal and beauty are attached to youth.

- Our throwaway society sequesters the dying. We see death as horrible. Children are kept from seeing death because it is deemed too hard for them. (Actually, children want to talk about death and understand what they already know.) Many adults lie about, avoid, and are ashamed by the reality that we will return to the dust.

Unhealthy shame occurs when we cling to the lies associated with our return to dust instead of holding fast to God's grace and mercy. For example, we might believe that our mortality is the result of being formed from the dust, but that is false. Scripture declares that our mortality is God's punishment for Adam and Eve's sin. We might believe that God removes Himself from us when we are suffering, while He clearly states in His Word that He seeks us out and finds us where we hide. We might believe that dying and death are ugly and shameful, but the Bible declares that a profound aliveness is at work, bringing wholeness and complete healing in Christ, despite what we see externally.

Ponder this simple example of dust in our homes. We live with a bit of dust each day. We put up with it and deal with it as regularly as possible. Before guests arrive, we dust and clean in preparation, and we do not see the dust. Something different occurs when guests stop by unannounced. Because we have not prepared beforehand, we are aware of our dust. Our guests probably see our dust too. We may choose to ignore it and hope that they do the same. We may choose to call ourselves out, saying, "I'm so embarrassed about this dust." We may also say, "I'm guilty, I haven't cleaned for a while." Our guest may say, "Don't worry about it; dust is such a bother."

However, if our guest harshly states, "Shame on *you!* Your home is filthy. Don't you ever clean?!" we feel shame. Shame says, "Not only is the dust wrong, but you are wrong." We want to crawl into a hole and hide. We may make excuses. Others have the power to make us feel ashamed, but only if we give that power to them. Even more challenging to overcome is the "shame on *me*" mentality that some of us practice. Many of us have lived in shame our entire lives because of hard words, merciless words of people who have influence in our lives. Shame gets in the way; shame may lead to despair of life itself.

We are not wrong for simply being alive, which is the unhealthy attitude of shame. We learned that attitude somewhere, but certainly not from a God who holds us in His mercy and grace. Acknowledging our guilt before God is good and right. Acknowledging the lies that lead to shame is also good and right. Separating those emotions and feelings helps us grow in our understanding of God's work for us and in us.

God sought Adam and Eve in the garden. When He found them, He asked, "Who told you that you were naked? Have you eaten of the tree of which I commanded you not to eat?" (Genesis 3:11). He asked these questions to invite them to receive mercy. When God found Adam and Eve, He did *not* declare, "Shame on you." God spoke to them exactly what He had promised: a return to the dust.

Guilt is a healthy, God-given emotion that affords us the opportunity to turn from disobedience to repentance and then to receive forgiveness. Shame does not come from God. Shame is an unhealthy emotion directly related to believing that we are disgraced. Shame leads to a sinful belief that we are removed from God's grace by what we think, say, do, or don't do. Yes, we are guilty, and the Law points us to own our guilt. But we are not shameful.

Healthy guilt says, "Adam and Eve's sin brought the punishment of death, and we have certainly added to their sin with our own thoughts, words, and actions or lack of action." God sought us out and found us and spoke mercy into the broken relationship Adam and Eve caused. God has spoken grace and mercy into our guilt. We take responsibility for our actions, recognize our guilt before God, repent, and receive His declaration of righteousness through His Son.

Dying and death are not shameful. Being alive is not shameful. Returning to dust is not shameful. Hiding from God and others in shame for feeling diminished value as we age adds to the same list of actions that Adam and Eve committed in the Garden of Eden. We may engage in some form of hiding: denying, blaming, covering up, and lying. Hiding from our own fears about the reality of our return to dust leads to anger, resentment, bitterness.[1]

We are called to acknowledge with eyes wide open that our bones will return to dust as a result of the punishment God declared on Adam and Eve. We are also called to recognize that just as God formed Adam from dust and breathed life into him, God formed us and breathes the breath of life in us. We have become and continue to become more fully alive by His creative breath.

FROM DUST TO LIVING

Scripture reflects a tension about life, dust, and living. We journey from dust to life, from life to dust, and from dust to living. Let's review: Adam was created from the dust to life by the breath of God. Adam disobeyed God, and God spoke punishment into that disobedience, which was Adam's return to dust. We inherited Adam's sin and God's punishment for it. We add to that original sin with our own. Christ, the Son of God, paid the price for Adam's disobedience and ours. Christ's perfect life lay in the dust for us. God breathes life into our being, and we live eternally now, in Christ, by the breath of God. Our bodies will return to the dust and—by the power of God—will be raised to reunite with our soul and spirit in the presence of God.

---

1 Shame and the anger, resentment, and bitterness that come from unhealthy shame are very complex. The Word of God speaks directly into our shame with love and mercy. At times, professional help may be needed to uncover and heal the deep wounds associated with the shame we feel. Please find a Christian therapist when you need help.

Living today and living for eternity, which are also present realities, is God's call on our lives. We hide in shame from the "I will return to the dust" fact, but again, dying is not a shameful event. Yet, to be afraid of dying and death is a natural response. Adam and Eve were created to live eternally. We were too; and when we see the effects of death around us and in our world, we can acknowledge that we inherited Adam and Eve's punishment.

Living means that we must face a temporary resting place in the dust where our flesh and bones will decay and return to the dust. Living eternally is God's plan for our lives; by His breath, we live even though our bodies return to the dust. Our bodies return to dust when we breathe our last breath on this earth. God's creative power keeps our soul and spirit in Him, which is the very place He has held us throughout our lives. Living means journeying into these truths today and growing in our understanding until we breathe our last.

Through breath and word, God bestows life to us as creatively, profoundly, and lovingly as He did at Adam's creation. Ponder this: just as we could not possibly shape a pile of dust or breathe it into a human life, neither can we breathe life and eternity into our lives. Life originates in the Creator, the breath of life, and is sustained by the Creator.

- LORD, You have been our dwelling place in all generations. Before the mountains were brought forth, or ever You had formed the earth and the world, from everlasting to everlasting You are God. **You return man to dust** and say, "Return, O children of man!" For a thousand years in Your sight are but as yesterday when it is past, or as a watch in the night. . . . So teach us to number our days that we may get a heart of wisdom. Psalm 90:1–4, 12 (emphasis added)

- He does not deal with us according to our sins, nor repay us according to our iniquities. For as high as the heavens are above the earth, so great is His steadfast love toward those who fear Him; as far as the east is from the west, so far does He remove our transgressions from us. As a father shows compassion to his children, so the Lord shows compassion to those who fear Him. For He knows our frame; **He remembers that we are dust.** Psalm 103:10–14 (emphasis added)

- These all look to You, to give them their food in due season. When You give it to them, they gather it up; when You open Your hand, they are filled with good things. When You hide Your face, they are dismayed; when You take away their breath, **they die and return to their dust.** When You send forth Your Spirit, they are created, and You renew the face of the ground. Psalm 104:27–30 (emphasis added)

The apostle Paul wrote to the people of Corinth, who were being told that there was no resurrection of the body from the dust. Paul begged believers to open their eyes to God's handiwork through the dust and breath:

So is it with the resurrection of the dead. What is sown is perishable; what is raised is imperishable. It is sown in dishonor; it is raised in glory. It is sown in weakness; it is raised in power. It is sown a natural body; it is raised a spiritual body. If there is a natural body, there is also a spiritual body. Thus it is written, "The first man Adam became a living being"; the last Adam became a life-giving spirit. But it is not the spiritual that is first but the natural, and then the spiritual. The first man was from the earth, a man of dust; the second man is from heaven. As was the man of dust, so also are those who are of the dust, and as is the man of heaven, so also are those who are of heaven. Just as we have borne the image of the man of dust, we shall also bear the image of the man of heaven. 1 Corinthians 15:42–49

Adam was a man of the dust, created in the image of God. Adam's actions of disobedience were not life-giving; rather, they brought punishment and death. Christ was a man from heaven. Every action Christ took was life-giving. Paul calls our attention to this very important distinction as he compares Adam and Christ. The sinless Son of God took on Adam's sin and ours in order that we might live through Him.

Living means so much more than having a human body with a beating heart and breathing lungs. Living means being fully alive, a complete human being as God intended. Our redemption through Christ's blood sealed that for us and made that which was impossible possible in His holy life. Our Creator redeemed our hearts and created a holy dwelling place for His Son. His breath breathes life into our being each and every moment and continues even when we breathe our last breath on this earth.

The dust of the earth that we see and touch teaches us that we are so much more than dust and that living is so much more than our eventual return to the dust. Dust also teaches us that we cannot create life out of lifelessness. We have no power within us to form life or breathe life into ourselves or anyone else. We must fully rely on our Creator, our Redeemer, and the Spirit of life to call us from dust to life.

The story of Christ's resurrection from the tomb will help us explore living and the contrast between the man from the dust and the Man from heaven. Exploring this story will also help us understand how even people of great faith who walked with Jesus and heard His promise that He would not remain in the grave sought Him among the dead because they thought He would be in the grave.

On the first day of the week, at early dawn, they went to the tomb, taking the spices they had prepared. And they found the stone rolled away from the tomb, but when they went in they did not find the body of the Lord Jesus. While they were perplexed about this, behold, two men stood by them in dazzling apparel. And as they were frightened and bowed their faces to the ground, the men said to them, "Why do you seek the living among the dead? He is not here, but has risen. Remember how He told you, while He was still in Galilee, that the Son of Man must be delivered into the hands of sinful men and be crucified and on the third day rise." Luke 24:1–7

The angel asked an important question: "Why do you seek the living among the dead?" A man from the dust would have been lying right where he had been laid upon death. However, the Man from heaven, who had come to earth in human skin, was not in the tomb where they had laid Him. The only place the women and disciples looked for Jesus' body was exactly where He told them He would not be. Luke continued:

And they remembered His words, and returning from the tomb they told all these things to the eleven and to all the rest. Now it was Mary Magdalene and Joanna and Mary the mother of James and the other women with them who told these things to the apostles, but these words seemed to them an idle tale, and they did not believe them. But Peter rose and ran to the tomb; stooping and looking in, he saw the linen cloths by themselves; and he went home marveling at what had happened. Luke 24:8–12

When Adam and Eve hid, God asked, "Who told you that you were naked? Have you eaten of the tree of which I commanded you not to eat?" (Genesis 3:11). Adam and Eve chose to look for life through the promise of the crafty serpent rather than through the promises of God. Dust reminds us just how easy it is to look for the promise of life precisely where God declared life would not be—among death.

Dust reminds us just how easy it is to hide in shame, to blame, lie, and ignore the fact that our bodies will return to the dust. Dying and death are not shameful; dying and death are part of the journey of living in this world after the Fall. Jesus promised that He would not be in the tomb, and Scripture clearly states that life is not in the tomb. Christ came to defeat death. Life is in Christ—now, in every stage of life, and for eternity. Our life doesn't end in the dust. Our physical body returns to dust after death, but it is resurrected into eternal life, while our soul and spirit rest in Christ now and for all eternity.

We marvel because the living Lord grants us life and calls our focus to be on Him, on His creative word and work in our lives. God seeks us; God finds us; God calls us to deeper faith in His plan, His mercy, and His love. At times, we try to live by this world's definition of life, living, youth, and beauty. God asks, "Why do you seek life and living here?" God says, "Living takes place through Me. Living is My gift to you, through My forming, My breath, My restoration, My putting you where you are at this time, in this place." God says, "Take courage and hope. Your return to dust is temporary; it is not shameful."

Dust settles; but we will not settle for less than life and living, which God intends for us. God breathes life into our lives and we become living beings more fully. We are called to trust in God and His word of the promise of life and living. We are called to throw off unhealthy shame and all the harsh actions and attitudes connected to it. Faith and trust acknowledge that our Savior paid for our guilt. Freedom from death and the dust is God's full desire for us. Paul declared, "If the Spirit of Him who raised Jesus from the dead dwells in you, He who raised Christ Jesus from the dead will also give life to your mortal bodies through His Spirit who dwells in you" (Romans 8:11).

God breathed life into the formed dust of Adam's lifeless body. That same miracle of life is ours today, through the dust, through forming, through breathing. With courage, authenticity, and hope, we face our fears. Each day, we grow in faith and trust in God's mercy and love for us and in us. We neither ignore our return to dust nor embrace dust as final our resting place. We learn from the dust that we have been redeemed from it, and we are living beings by God's Word and breath.

For individual study, meditate on the following questions and additional verses. For small-group study, discuss these questions:

1. What has dust revealed to you through these pages? What additional thoughts or Scripture verses came to your mind and heart as you meditated on these words?

2. Write your fears in the dust on your furniture or car (make sure you don't scratch your belongings). Give them to God in prayer and then wipe them clean. What did you learn about yourself through the process?

3. Read and meditate on Romans 6:1–14 and Romans 8:1–11 in light of freedom in Christ from the condemnation of death and dust.

Chapter Two

SAND

We continue our journey into *The Rock Speaks* with sand, which is a small particle of rock. The Pacific Ocean is only thirty miles west of Paso Robles, California, so a trip to the beach to play in the sand is a common occurrence for my family. I have fond memories of looking at the tide chart with my dad the evening before abalone-gathering expeditions. We'd wake up early, grab the gear we had packed the night before, and drive to Morro Bay. We'd park, gather our sacks and knives, and then head out, fully clothed, into the cold water. Abalone was plentiful in the 1960s, so we would limit out in a short time.

I also remember, not so fondly, shivering in the cold, damp fog as I undressed next to the pickup. Sand was everywhere! My jeans and socks felt like sandpaper as Dad helped me pull them off and change into dry clothes. The fun of the preparation and expedition gave way to the long ride home, sitting and squirming in the sand that stuck to my little body. When I finally took a bath, the bottom of the tub was covered with tiny grains of sand.

Majestic Morro Rock,
Morro Bay, California.

When I was a child, the dry creek bed behind my home was my playground. My brother and I climbed the clay cliffs, gathered rocks, and made forts with them. We'd sift the fine sand through the kitchen strainers Mom let us play with. My favorite times were after rainstorms that made the creek run. After the water subsided, fresh sand was exposed. The sand had a crispy crust, which we would break through with our fingers as we wrote our names in the sand.

Sand takes many forms in our modern world and is a resource used extensively in modern buildings and manufacturing. Glass is 70 to 75 percent sand in a highly modified form. Concrete is anywhere between 20 and 50 percent sand. Asphalt is 8 to 20 percent sand. Adobe bricks are 70 to 75 percent sand. In order to produce any of these strong, resilient materials, a proper ratio of sand to the other materials is critical. Heat is applied to sand to make glass and asphalt; water is mixed with sand and cement to make concrete.

Sand in glass form surrounds us! Whether in our homes, a hotel, or a fifty-story high-rise office complex, the windows are at least 70 percent silica sand. Car, train, bus, and plane windows are the same.

Sand in concrete and asphalt form is everywhere! Concrete forms the foundations of most modern buildings and forms the walls of many buildings. Concrete sidewalks and patios are part of our everyday lives. Concrete is used to build swimming pools. Concrete in the form of mortar is placed between bricks (which are 70 to 75 percent sand) to build homes, fireplaces, and decorative structures. Our highways, city streets, and country roads are 8 to 20 percent sand. Wherever we drive, we are driving on sand in some form.

Sand can be added to paint to create a nonslip surface for stairs and floors. Sand is used to cushion play areas. Sandpaper is used to prepare wood for a finishing coat of stain or paint. Sand bags are used as doorstops, gun rests, flood barriers, and weights. Sandblasting is a process used to remove paint or debris from objects. Sand is formed to create molds used in foundries for casting steel. Quartz sand, known as silica, is the primary ingredient in silicone.

The uses for sand are beyond imagination, and ingenuity and innovation will continue to drive the creation of products from sand for our modern world. Human ingenuity, while magnificent, cannot compare to our Creator's creation of sand, as we will consider as we explore the magnitude of His words of hope and mercy through sand.

As Numerous As the Sand: Children of Promise

Abraham and Sarah, in their old age, were promised a son. That promise was fulfilled when they gave birth to and raised a son, Isaac. Isaac was certainly old enough to know what was going on when Abraham was building an altar and placing wood on it, because he asked, "Where is the lamb for the sacrifice?" Abraham answered, "God will provide the lamb for this sacrifice," and then he placed Isaac, his only son, on the altar. God stopped Abraham—knife in midair to sacrifice his son as God had commanded—and provided a ram for the sacrifice.

Abraham called the place "God will provide." These verses include the angel's words to the faithful Abraham:

> And the angel of the LORD called to Abraham a second time from heaven and said, "By Myself I have sworn, declares the LORD, because you have done this and have not withheld your son, your only son, I will surely bless you, and I will surely multiply your offspring as the stars of heaven and as the sand that is on the seashore. And your offspring shall possess the gate of his enemies, and in your

offspring shall all the nations of the earth be blessed, because you have obeyed My voice." Genesis 22:15–18

I am in awe of Abraham's faith and obedience. He didn't question
God's command; he fulfilled it, even after all of the years of clinging to
God's promise of a family:

> The LORD said to Abram, after Lot had separated from him,
> "Lift up your eyes and look from the place where you are,
> northward and southward and eastward and westward, for
> all the land that you see I will give to you and to your off-
> spring forever. I will make your offspring as the dust of the
> earth, so that if one can count the dust of the earth, your
> offspring also can be counted." Genesis 13:14–16

The author of Hebrews, in the great chapter 11 on the faith of the
patriarchs, said this about Abraham:

> By faith Abraham obeyed when he was called to go out
> to a place that he was to receive as an inheritance. And
> he went out, not knowing where he was going. By faith he
> went to live in the land of promise, as in a foreign land,
> living in tents with Isaac and Jacob, heirs with him of the
> same promise. For he was looking forward to the city that
> has foundations, whose designer and builder is God. By
> faith Sarah herself received power to conceive, even when
> she was past the age, since she considered Him faithful
> who had promised. Therefore from one man, and him as
> good as dead, were born descendants as many as the stars
> of heaven and as many as the innumerable grains of sand
> by the seashore. Hebrews 11:8–12

We are the inheritors of the promise! St. Paul says, "Christ redeemed
us from the curse of the law by becoming a curse for us—for it is written,

'Cursed is everyone who is hanged on a tree'—so that in Christ Jesus the blessing of Abraham might come to the Gentiles, so that we might receive the promised Spirit through faith" (Galatians 3:13–14).

We, the children of the promise, are the "innumerable grains of sand" described so many generations ago. Abraham rested in the promises and mercy of God. His life is held up for us not because he was perfect and did everything perfectly, but because he lived in faith. We rest in the promises and mercy of God; we live in Christ, trusting His perfection as the fulfillment of God's promise to sacrifice the perfect Lamb, His one and only Son.

Abraham declared, and we declare too, "God will provide." With Abraham, Isaac, and all those in the family who have gone before us, we also declare, "God has provided the perfect Lamb." The provision—an inheritance, if you will—is a gift, a land of promise that is both now and not yet. We are inheritors of all of the promises of God, and we will enjoy perfect fulfillment of all of them, for us, for all eternity.

As Numerous As the Sand: Precious Thoughts of God

Human words cannot possibly express the quantity of sand on this earth. Likewise, human words cannot possibly express the quantity of the thoughts of God toward us. Exploring the thoughts of God begins with David's psalm: "How precious to me are Your thoughts, O God! How vast is the sum of them! If I would count them, they are more than the sand. I awake, and I am still with You" (Psalm 139:17–18).

Before we explore the precious, innumerable thoughts of God, let's pause for a moment and wrestle with the concept of "the thoughts of God." Our limited human minds and understanding cannot possibly fathom the way God thinks. As we just read in the previous paragraph, David compared the vast, precious thoughts of God to the incomprehensible number of grains of sand. The prophet Isaiah conveyed God's thoughts, and he calls us to a deeper understanding of the thoughts of God in this way:

> Seek the LORD while He may be found; call upon Him while He is near; let the wicked forsake his way, and the unrighteous man his thoughts; let him return to the LORD, that He may have compassion on him, and to our God, for He will abundantly pardon. For My thoughts are not your thoughts, neither are your ways My ways, declares the LORD. For as the heavens are higher than the earth, so are My ways higher than your ways and My thoughts than your thoughts. Isaiah 55:6–9

The thoughts of God are not our thoughts; the thoughts of God are higher than our thoughts. Human imagination is appropriate when inventing uses for sand and is important for pondering the number of grains of sand on the seashore. However, imagination must take a backseat when meditating on the thoughts of God.

Surfers resting on the sand, Newport Beach, California.

God calls us to rely on His Word, not our imagination, to explore His thoughts. The Word of God, inspired by the Spirit of God and written by the people of God, communicates to us the thoughts of God. The apostle Paul says no one can comprehend the thoughts of God except the Spirit of God, and that only by the Spirit of God in us can we understand the gifts of God:

> As it is written, "What no eye has seen, nor ear heard, nor the heart of man imagined, what God has prepared for those who love Him"—these things God has revealed to us through the Spirit. For the Spirit searches everything, even the depths of God. For who knows a person's thoughts except the spirit of that person, which is in him? So also no one comprehends the thoughts of God except the Spirit of God. Now we have received not the spirit of the world, but the Spirit who is from God, that we might understand the things freely given us by God. 1 Corinthians 2:9–12

The precious thoughts of God toward us are as innumerable as the grains of sand, which God created—and there is so much more. God's thoughts don't change on a whim. God's thoughts are not dependent upon our thoughts toward Him or our actions toward our neighbor. God created us; God's Son, with His holy, precious blood, restored the broken relationship with God. God's Spirit dwells in us by His very breath and calls us to deeper faith and trust in the triune God.

The precious, vast thoughts of God toward us are perfect and are based solely in His perfection, righteousness, and mercy. David proclaims these powerful words for us:

> Blessed is the man who makes the LORD his trust, who does not turn to the proud, to those who go astray after a lie! You have multiplied, O LORD my God, Your wondrous

deeds and Your thoughts toward us; none can compare with You! I will proclaim and tell of them, yet they are more than can be told. Psalm 40:4–5

May all who seek You rejoice and be glad in You; may those who love Your salvation say continually, "Great is the LORD!" As for me, I am poor and needy, but the LORD takes thought for me. You are my help and my deliverer; do not delay, O my God! Psalm 40:16–17

As we explore the innumerable thoughts of God toward us, it is critical that we take some time to consider our thoughts toward Him, our thoughts toward our neighbor, and our thoughts toward ourselves. While we know that God's thoughts are not dependent upon our thoughts, we wrestle with truly believing that. Paul knew this, and so he calls us to practice thinking in this way:

Finally, brothers, whatever is true, whatever is honorable, whatever is just, whatever is pure, whatever is lovely, whatever is commendable, if there is any excellence, if there is anything worthy of praise, think about these things. What you have learned and received and heard and seen in me— practice these things, and the God of peace will be with you. Philippians 4:8–9

We are not accustomed to steadfast, pure thoughts in our very challenging, fast-paced modern world. Noise surrounds us and many, many distractions pull us in different directions. The sheer speed of life causes our thoughts to race. The moods of people around us can be fickle. Our inner voice often speaks harshly of ourselves, others, and even God. Many of us struggle with our thoughts, especially when we're alone. We attempt to soothe ourselves by trying to ignore our thoughts or fill our mind with noise or forms of medication.

- What do we do? We are not called to dwell in our harsh thoughts, but we must, in honesty, recognize our inner thoughts. God created us with the need to express—not bury—our thoughts, emotions, and feelings. Feelings and emotions are not wrong, but many of us were taught otherwise. When we bury our emotions and feelings, we suppress an important part of our created being.

Here is one example. Anger is not wrong. Improper expression of anger is wrong; rage is wrong. Many of us were taught that being angry with God is wrong, so we try to bury that anger. We try to force ourselves to think only the thoughts we think we "should" think toward God—and that backfires. We end up in a vicious circle and horrible mind game because we believe we're not supposed to think "that way." Yet God's desire for us is freedom as vast as the grains of sand on the shore.

God can certainly handle all of our thoughts toward Him, and so we dig into the Psalms to challenge our thinking about our thoughts toward God.

- My soul thirsts for God, for the living God. When shall I come and appear before God? My tears have been my food day and night, while they say to me all the day long, "Where is your God?" . . . I say to God, my rock: "Why have You forgotten me? Why do I go mourning because of the oppression of the enemy?" As with a deadly wound in my bones, my adversaries taunt me, while they say to me all the day long, "Where is your God?" Psalm 42:2–3, 9–10

- I am weary with my crying out; my throat is parched. My eyes grow dim with waiting for my God. Psalm 69:3

- You have caused my companions to shun me; You have made me a horror to them. I am shut in so that I cannot escape; my eye grows dim through sorrow. Every day I call upon You, O LORD; I spread out my hands to You. Do You work wonders for the dead? Do the departed rise up to praise You? . . . But I, O LORD, cry to You; in the morning my prayer comes before You. O LORD, why do You cast my soul away? Why do You hide Your face from me? Psalm 88:8–10, 13–14

- Out of the depths I cry to You, O LORD! O LORD, hear my voice! Let Your ears be attentive to the voice of my pleas for mercy! Psalm 130:1–2

Do we give ourselves permission to cry out to God from the depths of our hearts, realizing that it is an act of faith to share our deepest thoughts, emotions, and feelings—including anger—with Him? In the face of extreme challenge, such as loss of loved ones or illness or injury or natural disaster or abandonment, do we give ourselves permission to express our heart to God? Or do we swallow our negative emotions and try to limit our thinking toward God to what we believe we are supposed to think?

We are called to explore this aspect of our thinking for the purpose of more fully understanding the precious, "as vast as the grains of sand" thoughts of God toward us. Consider this in the context of anger: Many have been taught that anger is wrong and that being angry with God is wrong. Yet if we learned that we can't be angry with God, then we can most certainly learn the opposite: that it is okay to be angry with God. While it is certainly uncomfortable, we can learn to express our anger toward God. It will take time to relearn the truth because the incorrect teaching is ingrained and we've practiced it for so long.

If we are confused about healthy anger and unhealthy anger (rage), then we will be confused about the thoughts of God, including His anger toward sin, evil, and injustice. God calls us to live fully, and that includes understanding our thoughts about ourselves, others, and Him. God can handle our thoughts, all of them. He calls us to authenticity and genuine hearts of faith in Him. David declared:

> O LORD, You have searched me and known me! You know when I sit down and when I rise up; You discern my thoughts from afar. You search out my path and my lying down and are acquainted with all my ways. Even before a word is on my tongue, behold, O LORD, You know it altogether. You hem me in, behind and before, and lay Your hand upon me. Such knowledge is too wonderful for me; it is high; I cannot attain it. Psalm 139:1–6

God's thoughts toward sin, evil, and injustice are articulated clearly in the Scriptures. Interpreting those words must be done from a clear understanding of Adam's disobedience, God's punishment, and God's mercy. To repentant hearts, the God of the Old Testament, Jesus, and the apostles of the New Testament spoke only mercy and forgiveness. Individuals with unrepentant, hard hearts received the righteous anger, wrath, and justice of God.

Look at the sand on the lakeshore and seashore, riverbed and desert. Count the tiny grains. The precious, innumerable thoughts of God toward us are more than all of that combined. Look through your windows, crafted of sand, and see the precious thoughts of God toward you. Stand on the cement of your patio and ponder the sand beneath your feet. Embrace God's precious thoughts for you as the foundation of life—and live!

WISDOM BEYOND MEASURE, LIKE THE SAND ON THE SEASHORE

Sand also reminds us of God's interactions with Solomon. God appeared to Solomon in a dream and said, "Ask!" Solomon asked for an understanding mind and a discerning heart; Solomon asked for wisdom. Here is the story:

> At Gibeon the LORD appeared to Solomon in a dream by night, and **God said, "Ask what I shall give you."** And Solomon said, "You have shown great and steadfast love to Your servant David my father, because he walked before You in faithfulness, in righteousness, and in uprightness of heart toward You. And You have kept for him this great and steadfast love and have given him a son to sit on his throne this day. And now, O LORD my God, You have made Your servant king in place of David my father, although I am but a little child. I do not know how to go out or come in. And Your servant is in the midst of Your people whom You have chosen, a great people, too many to be numbered or counted for multitude. **Give Your servant therefore an understanding mind to govern Your people, that I may discern between good and evil, for who is able to govern this Your great people?"**
>
> It pleased the LORD that Solomon had asked this. And God said to him, "Because you have asked this, and have not asked for yourself long life or riches or the life of your enemies, but have asked for yourself understanding to discern what is right, behold, I now do according to your word. **Behold, I give you a wise and discerning mind, so that none like you has been before you and none like you shall arise after you."** 1 Kings 3:5–12 (emphasis added)
>
> **God gave Solomon wisdom and understanding beyond measure, and breadth of mind like the sand on the seashore,** so that Solomon's wisdom surpassed the wisdom of all the people of the east and all the wisdom of Egypt.

... And people of all nations came to hear the wisdom of Solomon, and from all the kings of the earth, who had heard of his wisdom. 1 Kings 4:29–30, 34 (emphasis added)

We are beneficiaries of Solomon's heartfelt request to God for wisdom. His thoughts on God and life live on through the books of the Bible he wrote. Read a few of my favorite passages from those books, and then highlight your own as you reflect.

- Trust in the LORD with all your heart, and do not lean on your own understanding. In all your ways acknowledge Him, and He will make straight your paths. Be not wise in your own eyes; fear the LORD, and turn away from evil. It will be healing to your flesh and refreshment to your bones. Proverbs 3:5–8

- The fear of the LORD is the beginning of wisdom, and the knowledge of the Holy One is insight. Proverbs 9:10

- Train up a child in the way he should go; even when he is old he will not depart from it. Proverbs 22:6

- To know wisdom and instruction, to understand words of insight, to receive instruction in wise dealing, in righteousness, justice, and equity; to give prudence to the simple, knowledge and discretion to the youth—Let the wise hear and increase in learning, and the one who understands obtain guidance, to understand a proverb and a saying, the words of the wise and their riddles. The fear of the LORD is the beginning of knowledge; fools despise wisdom and instruction. Proverbs 1:2–7

- Keep your heart with all vigilance, for from it flow the springs of life. Proverbs 4:23

- Iron sharpens iron, and one man sharpens another. Proverbs 27:17

- Every word of God proves true; He is a shield to those who take refuge in Him. Proverbs 30:5

We marvel at Solomon's wisdom, and we would be wise to study, reflect, and learn from his words. We also marvel at Solomon's request for wisdom from God. God invited Solomon to request anything—yes, *anything!* God said, "Ask what I shall give you." We wish God would give us that same opportunity. Yet, He has and does! God invites us to ask for wisdom. God invites us to ask Him what to ask. God invites us to listen to our free hearts, knowing that His thoughts are for us, and ask.

Do we have the courage to speak our hearts and to ask? Jesus has so much more in store for us, so much more than the grains of sand on the seashore. Following are some of the times Jesus invited us to ask:

- To the woman at the well, Jesus said, "If you knew the gift of God, and who it is that is saying to you, 'Give me a drink,' you would have asked Him, and He would have given you living water" (John 4:10). Jesus asked for a sip of water; Jesus invited the woman to ask for living water. Jesus not only invited her to ask for the gift, He also promised the giving. Think about the gift of living water and the life-giving thoughts of God toward us. Living water is infinite, unfathomable in its capacity to bring life and healing and wholeness; the thoughts of God toward us are infinite, as the sands of the seashore, and they are life-giving.

- Jesus, in His infinite wisdom, invited His followers to ask. The apostles in the Upper Room received a foot washing, a message about Jesus' coming death and resurrection, and

Jesus declared, "I am the true vine." During the Upper Room interactions, Jesus also invited:

— Whatever you **ask** in My name, this I will do, that the Father may be glorified in the Son. John 14:13

— If you **ask** me anything in My name, I will do it. John 14:14

— If you abide in Me, and My words abide in you, **ask** whatever you wish, and it will be done for you. John 15:7

— You did not choose Me, but I chose you and appointed you that you should go and bear fruit and that your fruit should abide, so that whatever you **ask** the Father in My name, He may give it to you. John 15:16

— In that day you will ask nothing of Me. Truly, truly, I say to you, whatever you **ask** of the Father in My name, He will give it to you. Until now you have asked nothing in My name. **Ask**, and you will receive, that your joy may be full. John 16:23–24

— In that day you will **ask** in My name, and I do not say to you that I will ask the Father on your behalf; for the Father Himself loves you, because you have loved Me and have believed that I came from God. John 16:26–27

Jesus drew the apostles into relationship during the three years that He walked with them. The struggles they faced by answering His call to follow pale in comparison to the events of Jesus' betrayal, arrest, trial, crucifixion, and burial. Jesus' offer to "ask anything in My name" was not whimsical, nor was His invitation to ask spoken at a time of great calm and peace.

Jesus' invitation to ask is intimately tied to the relationship we have with Him. He calls, equips, leads; we listen, follow, and ask. The fellowship we have with Christ, through His Word and work, precedes and frames our asking. The intimacy we share with Him—an eternity in His life—gives us confidence to do what He invites us to do: ask anything of the Father in His name.

Jesus requested many things of His Father, yet there was one request that His Father did not fulfill: "Take this cup from Me." Matthew records, "And going a little farther He fell on His face and prayed, saying, 'My Father, if it be possible, let this cup pass from Me; nevertheless, not as I will, but as You will'" (Matthew 26:39). God did not take suffering and death away from Jesus, and Jesus accepted that He must endure the cross and the grave. Jesus knew it was His Father's will to work through His crucifixion and death to restore God's relationship with us.

Our life is filled with hardships—some of our own doing, some of other's actions toward us, and some the result of original sin—that we would like taken from us. God hears our earnest prayers to take our crosses from us according to His good and gracious will. Sometimes those crosses are removed and sometimes not. In all circumstances, He invites us to gain wisdom and the courage to ask and to trust. We bear our crosses because we must, not because hardship was ever part of God's design. However, God will work through all things to bring us closer to Himself. And so, because God invites us to do so, we ask with full confidence that our requests are heard and answered according to the will of God. One of the most challenging crosses we will bear is our own death. God works through that cross too, bringing life fully through our death.

Christ's death led to life for us. I wonder if the disciples ever asked God to raise Jesus from the dead. Did they even think to ask it? Did they think it possible? Did they resign themselves to the grave as final? I believe that John considered this and many other questions for the fifty to sixty years following Jesus' ascension before he authored his Gospel. John asked

God to reveal just the right words to write about life in Christ for our benefit. In this context, then, how do *we* ask? We ask with boldness, confidence, and eyes wide open to the infinite possibilities of God.

Sand, the innumerable grains of sand, reminds us that God's thoughts toward us are consistent, infinitely kind, and filled with love and grace. Sand reminds us that Jesus invited the apostles and invites us to ask— without limitation. The invitation to ask is grounded in relationship, grounded in understanding that the triune God, the giver, has infinite, precious thoughts toward us, the askers and receivers of His gifts.

For individual study, meditate on the following questions. For small-group study, discuss these questions:

1. What has sand revealed to you through these pages? What additional thoughts or Scripture verses came to your mind and heart as you meditated on these words?

2. Ponder why it is so easy, in the face of extreme challenge, to believe God's thoughts toward us have changed. Meditate on God's precious thoughts toward you!

3. What do you wish? What do you hope? Humbly ask God for what you want!

Grandma's Hill towers over Steinbeck Vineyards.

Chapter Three

SOIL OF THE GROUND

The ground of the earth and the soil of the ground will be our topics to discover in this chapter of *The Rock Speaks*. The ground and the soil of the ground vary dramatically in every region of the world. Fertile soils of the ground are chosen for human habitation, for growing food and fiber. Much of the ground on this earth is not suited for agriculture and is uninhabitable. The magnitude, the layers, and the abundance of types of ground and soil are beyond comprehension or imagination.

In Steinbeck Vineyards, there are as many as forty classifiable soil types. When people ask, we say that our topsoils are primarily sandy loam and clay. The layers under the topsoil include shale, decomposed granite, and mudstone. We use very general terms to classify the very complex soils. Soil experts use scientific names and classifications.

The ground and soil—"dirt"—were our playground when my brother and I were children. Playing in the dirt entertained us for hours on end, days on end. We dug in the cliff banks, climbed the banks, made dirt clod forts, dug deep holes, made mud pies, sifted soil through our fingers, and,

I'm sure (but don't remember), threw dirt and mud at each other. We were fascinated when Dad was covered by dirt after a day's work on the tractor. Dad would say, "I played in the dirt all day!"

The fertile soil adjacent to my home has yielded garden vegetables for me and my neighbors for many years. Each spring, I till the soil, add amendments, lay irrigation lines, and plant seeds or starts. A few weeks later, I enjoy squash, cucumbers, tomatoes, and many other veggies. My garden also hosts volunteer vegetables, plants that sprout from last year's seeds that have been lying dormant or seeds that were in the compost or even in bird droppings.

The soil, when irrigated, also yields many and varied weeds. As unwelcome as they are in my garden, I learn from them. The soil holds the weed seeds, and when water is added, they sprout and take root. The abundance of the garden is amazing; the abundance of weeds is, well, less than desirable. When asked, "Do you grow anything other than grapes on your property?" Dad answers, "Weeds!" We chuckle, but the truth is that a large portion of the work and expense of operating our vineyard is getting rid of weeds.

Preparing the soil is different for different crops. Shallow-rooted annual garden veggies need only topsoil, the first few inches of soil, to grow. Grapevine roots make their way deep into the soil, as much as twenty feet. Before planting my vegetable garden, I cultivate the soil six to eight inches deep with a garden tiller. Before planting a vineyard, when the field is bare, we rip the ground five feet deep in one direction and three feet deep diagonally across that with a large tractor (a Caterpillar D9 or D10) that chugs along at one mile per hour. The movement of the tractor combined with the deep blade ripping the ground feels like waves to the person standing nearby.

The soil is tilled in many ways. Cultivator points or disc blades turn the topsoil for the garden. Soil is also cultivated when I use a hoe or shovel to remove weeds or when I gently scratch the surface to allow seeds to push their way through. A ripper shank cuts through the hardpan and churns the soil in the vineyard. After we rip, we till the ground again to break up the bumpy soil, passing over it many times with varied implements, such as cultivator, disk, and float drag. Only after such labored preparation is the soil ready for building and planting the vineyard.

The abundance of food produced from the soil is magnificent! Grocery stores, farm stands, and farmers markets burst with brilliant colors of food that came from the ground.

Plants and trees grow roots down into the ground and produce vegetables, grains, and fruit above the ground. Other plants produce edible root crops in the soil—carrots, potatoes, and radishes, for example—while foliage grows out of the ground to draw nutrients from the sun and air.

Life cannot exist without soil; life is sustained by soil. Open the fridge or pantry and ponder how connected to the soil we are through food and drink. Dairy products and meat come from animals whose lives are sustained by food grown in the soil. Grains, such as corn, wheat, and rice, are the base product for most processed foods. Nuts grow on trees that are grown in soil. Oil is processed from plant and animal life. Honey is made by bees from the nectar of flowers of many plants. Seafood comes from the waters, which are held in place by the ground, and plant life grows on the floor of the body of water in the "soil."

The ground and soil provide a window for us into God's creative work. The ground and soil also provide an opportunity to explore Jesus' work as He walked on the earth He created. We don't need to be agriculturalists to grasp the vastness of God's mercy toward us through the ground of the earth and the soil of the ground from which life is sustained.

Up Out of the Ground

God spoke light and darkness into existence; God spoke the sun, moon, planets, and stars into existence; God spoke the ground and waters into existence. The thoughts of God and the words of God created the ground. God's creative work in creation gives us pause as we continue to marvel at His creative thoughts through the ground and through soil!

God's thoughts and words created the ground. God's creative thoughts and work were different for bringing forth vegetation, animal life, and human beings than they were for creating the ground. Here is the account from Genesis 2:

> When no bush of the field was yet in the land and no small plant of the field had yet sprung up—for the LORD God had not caused it to rain on the land, and there was no man to work the ground, and a mist was going up from the land and was watering the whole face of the ground—then the LORD God formed the man of dust from the ground and breathed into his nostrils the breath of life, and the man became a living creature. And the LORD God planted

a garden in Eden, in the east, and there He put the man whom He had formed. And out of the ground the LORD God made to spring up every tree that is pleasant to the sight and good for food. The tree of life was in the midst of the garden, and the tree of the knowledge of good and evil. Genesis 2:5–9

God created the ground by His word. The ground held seeds for every plant and tree we know. God sent moisture in the form of a mist coming up from the ground, and with that moisture every tree and plant sprung up out of the ground. Try to picture bare ground giving way to every plant and tree we know. I can only imagine this based on my experience.

I've seen the bare, dry fields planted with grains in November, then spring forth with tiny green sprouts after the first rains of winter. When the clouds give way to sunshine, the light glistens off the little shoots. It is a magnificent sight as the ground bears the fruit of the planted seeds. I've seen fallow soil sprout a wide variety of weeds from seeds that were lying dormant in the soil, just waiting for the rains and warmth of the sun.

The carefully chosen words of Moses in Genesis 2 reveal a God of intimacy and personal thought and touch. Scripture says that God planted the Garden of Eden for the human being He created from dust. Again, I can only imagine, based on my experience of planting my garden. I till the ground, map out the sections for different vegetables, buy seeds or starts, lay irrigation lines, and then plant my garden. How did God plant the Garden of Eden?

Scripture also says that God placed Adam, a living being, into the garden He had planted for a very special purpose. "The LORD God took the man and put him in the garden of Eden to work it and keep it" (Genesis 2:15). In addition to working and keeping the garden, God gave Adam this work: "Now out of the ground the LORD God had formed every beast of the field and every bird of the heavens and brought them to the man to see what he would call them. And whatever the man called every living creature, that was its name" (Genesis 2:19). He must have been a very busy man, filling his time caring for God's creation. Far more than just his job, keeping and naming was his holy calling—his vocation—given by God to fill his days. His vocation also included his relationship with God, walking and talking. When God gifted Adam and Eve with each other, Adam's vocation expanded to include his life in relationship with his wife. The two of them worked together, keeping the garden. God also called Adam and Eve to be fruitful, to multiply and fill the earth.

God's creative work gave Adam and Eve creative work. This has tremendous implications for us through the soil of the ground even now. Our life is a gift from our Creator. His creative work in us gives us creative work that is our calling, our vocation. Our vocation is our opportunity to express our uniqueness in this world, and it is life-sustaining work. That creative work is not limited to our job. Our callings are gifts from God, grounded in God's creative work. Included in our calling is our work of sustaining life, taking care of our physical needs through feeding our bodies with nutrition that comes from the soil.

Consider the following examples of our high calling from God, His very special gift to us where we are. This list is an example, a springboard for you to add to from your personal experience. Please be aware that our tendency is to judge some callings as higher than others, but God's Word does not support that thinking. God's Word makes no distinction; rather, Paul says, "For we are His workmanship, created in Christ Jesus for good works, which God prepared beforehand, that we should walk in them" (Ephesians 2:10).

God's call on our lives is that we find our value in being alive according to His creative work; our calling flows from being alive. Our callings breed life and freedom and an opportunity to say thank You to our heavenly Father for giving us life. This concept is simple, not simplistic, so have fun adding to this list in light of God's creative work!

- **Self.** Human beings are called to balance. Caring for all aspects of self are included in this list.

  — Physical needs include proper rest and nutrition, education and feeding of the mind, soul, and spirit, care of emotions and heart, and healthy boundaries, that is, being responsible for self and responsible to others.

  — Caring for ourselves is a high calling. There are times when we cannot fulfill that calling and others must care for us. Therefore, receiving is vocation too, and receiving care and being thankful for it is part of our vocation because God has given another the vocation of caring for us.

- **Others.** Human beings live in relationship to others and are called to balance in those relationships.

- **Family.** Being part of a family gives each person—mom, dad, child—opportunities to express vocation to others. Changing a baby's diaper, preparing meals, teaching a child to care for self, and husband and wife showing love and mercy are just a few examples. Single people are called by God to live holy lives in singleness and without creatively expressing their sexuality, while married people are called to creatively express their love with each other. These are high and holy callings according to God's design.

- **Home and belongings.** Caring for and being responsible with our finances is our holy calling. Caring for the place we live and for our belongings is our holy calling.

- **Work.** In our modern world, some get paid for their work while others volunteer. Retired folks live off the finances of their former work. Regardless, our work is designed by God to be an expression of ourselves and to be life-sustaining. At times work isn't pleasant, but it still gives us opportunity to live out our calling with thanksgiving.

Adam and Eve's calling was directly connected to the ground and to the soil. We may not see our vocation so directly connected, but it is because our lives are sustained by the soil. Vocation encompasses all of life, all of living in God's creation. Our hearts and hands and voices express our gratitude for life, for living. Living takes place through the ground and soil.

Reflecting while walking the Labyrinth.

DOWN TO THE GROUND

Adam was given a very, very long to-do list. Proportionately, his do-not-do list was very, very short. There was only one "don't." As we discussed in chapter 1, the "don't eat of the tree of knowledge of good and evil" gave Adam an opportunity to obey and to worship God. We also discussed Adam and Eve's relationship to the dust, to dying, and to death as a result of their disobedience.

God's command "Do not eat of the tree in the center of the garden" was related to Adam's life call to keep and to name. Adam and Eve were given freedom to touch, eat from, and care for every other tree in the garden. Their disobedience led to living outside the call of God; their disobedience was directly related to their vocation. Adam wasn't called to be God. Adam was called to be a human being and to care for God's creation.

This event teaches us that the greatest challenges and temptations we face are directly related to our callings in life. According to our calling in life, our to-do list is very long. In addition to the brief list above, God calls us to love Him, our self, and our neighbor; to live in harmony; and to serve—no small tasks! Freedom in Christ means freedom within our calling. God's very short do-not-do list for us as individuals relates specifically to our individual vocations. Obeying God's "don't" doesn't earn favor with God. Obedience is a form of worship, an act of praise.

Here is one example from Adam and Eve that helps us open our eyes to living within our calling and to the disobedience of living outside our calling: Adam and Eve were called to love, cherish, and cling to each other. When God approached them after their first act of disobedience, they turned on each other. They blamed each other rather than taking responsibility for themselves. They stepped outside their callings as husband and wife. They sinned. Their actions led to shame, and shame led to blame.

The profound effect of Adam and Eve's disobedience has many more implications for us, many of which are related to the ground. After disobeying God's command, God said to Adam:

> Because you have listened to the voice of your wife and have eaten of the tree of which I commanded you, "You shall not eat of it," cursed is the ground because of you; in pain you shall eat of it all the days of your life; thorns and thistles it shall bring forth for you; and you shall eat the plants of the field. By the sweat of your face you shall eat bread, till you return to the ground, for out of it you were taken; for you are dust, and to dust you shall return. Genesis 3:17–19

God sent Adam and Eve out of the Garden of Eden He had created just for them. They were sent out to work the ground, which He cursed as punishment for their disobedience. "The Lord God sent him out from the garden of Eden to work the ground from which he was taken" (Genesis 3:23). Because of their disobedience, we also work "by the sweat of [our] face." Today we may not directly work the ground in our vocation, but certainly we pay workers to work the ground for our daily sustenance. And, like Adam and Eve, we will return to the ground.

Adam's sons Cain and Abel provide another example of living within and outside one's calling. The brothers had different callings. Cain worked the ground; Abel kept sheep. Their offerings to God were given according to their callings—Cain offered fruit of the ground; Abel offered a lamb. Each, according to his calling, was to give with a pure heart to God out of gratitude for life. Yet Cain's offering was given out of obligation, while Abel's was given from a pure heart.

Cain murdered Abel, probably by striking him with a rock from the ground, out of anger, jealousy, and disappointment at God's response to his offering. His lack of worship and his disobedience led to his committing murder. Further, his subsequent sin mirrored his father's—Adam blamed Eve; Cain blamed Abel. God asked Cain, "Where is Abel your brother?" Cain said, "I do not know; am I my brother's keeper?" (Genesis 4:9). Yes; according to his calling as a brother, he was his brother's keeper. He was to love his brother, not murder his brother. Here is God's interaction with Cain:

> And the LORD said, "What have you done? The voice of your brother's blood is crying to Me from the ground. And now you are cursed from the ground, which has opened its mouth to receive your brother's blood from your hand. When you work the ground, it shall no longer yield to you its strength. You shall be a fugitive and a wanderer on the earth." Genesis 4:10–12

Abel's blood flowed down to the ground and cried up to God from the ground. God heard Abel's cry and took action. Cain's punishment for disobedience was that the ground "would no longer yield . . . its strength" and his life would be lived out wandering the earth. The punishment for Cain (as for Adam) mirrored his calling. He acted outside his calling and received punishment related to his calling.

God's promise, as always, was bigger than His punishment! God promised redemption through Adam and Eve—through a Son who would defeat the serpent. Jesus, the man, experienced temptation, trial, dying, and death, yet He was fully obedient to His calling. Jesus, our Redeemer, passed through the ground to redeem you and me—inheritors of Adam and Eve's disobedience and punishment AND inheritors of God's promise of mercy and grace.

The ground calls us to grasp in faith and bold confidence that Christ's sacrifice fulfilled God's promises. Christ bore our sin in His body and endured the cross and death in our place. Through the ground, God calls us to a deeper understanding of His mercy as He gave His only Son into the ground and called Him forth from the ground into life for us. The ground also calls us to live in mercy and forgiveness toward one another as we live in relationships in this world. The ground teaches this; the soil of the ground has even more.

Up Out of the Soil of the Ground

Life is sustained by food from the soil of the ground, a fact of God's creative design. We cannot live without nourishment for our bodies, and that nourishment has roots in the soil. Fruits, vegetables, nuts, and grains are grown in the soil; animals, reptiles, and birds eat food from the soil or creatures whose life has been sustained from the soil.

Modern conveniences of grocery stores distance us from soil. Many have not experienced picking a ripe plum, wiping away the dust, and eating it while standing in the soil under the tree. Many have not pulled a carrot, wiped it off, and crunched on it while standing in the soil from which it came. Many have not picked a ripe watermelon, split it open, and sat in the soil, eating its fruit while juice is dripping down hands and elbows.

If you ask a child who lives removed from the soil where fruit and veggies come from, he may answer, "The grocery store." The same would be true for milk and meat. Yet there's an increasing interest in food sources. Agritourism is a growing industry around the world, fueled by city dwellers who want to see where their food and fiber are produced. Agriculturalists welcome guests onto their farms to teach them about the soil and food production.

My family offers tours of our vineyard property so that people can have a behind-the-wines look at agriculture. We bounce around in an old Jeep over dusty roads and through the fields. A favorite time of the year is September and October, when we pick grapes from the vines. Our guests love tasting the fruit, getting sticky, a hands-on experience of the soil and wine.

People are hungry to know more about sustainable farming, I believe, because of a deep desire for living a sustainable life. God is at work through the soil to draw us to Himself. The soil of the ground illustrates this important concept. We don't need to be farmers to understand this desire for sustainable life, but we do need to comprehend that we came from the ground, are sustained by the ground, and will return to the ground. We need to know that the Giver of life, our Rock, called Himself the bread of life. Manna came down from heaven to feed the wandering children of Israel to sustain their lives; Christ, the bread of life, came down from heaven, walked the ground of this earth, and ate food from this earth in order to redeem and sustain our lives.

Jesus' parable of the soil and the seed includes different types of soil:

- the soil of a path where scattered seeds were trampled;

- rocks and shallow soil where there were no nutrients or water;

- good soil with weeds that choked the planted seeds; and

- good soil into which seed was planted that yielded a fruitful crop.

Jesus interpreted His words for His closest followers.

> Now the parable is this: The seed is the word of God. The ones along the path are those who have heard; then the devil comes and takes away the word from their hearts, so that they may not believe and be saved. And the ones on the rock are those who, when they hear the word, receive

it with joy. But these have no root; they believe for a while, and in time of testing fall away. And as for what fell among the thorns, they are those who hear, but as they go on their way they are choked by the cares and riches and pleasures of life, and their fruit does not mature. As for that in the good soil, they are those who, hearing the word, hold it fast in an honest and good heart, and bear fruit with patience. Luke 8:11–15

"The seed is the word of God." Jesus, the Word in the flesh, planted the seed in the hearts of the hearers—the good soil—who received, heard, and held fast the Word, then bore the fruit. We are hungry to grow in understanding as the seed of the Word of God works in our hearts. We embrace with patience the process of growing and bearing fruit.

Receiving Jesus through the Soil

In the story John tells us in John 9, the blind man received far more than the seed of the Word into his heart. He received mud on his eyes. Jesus spit on the ground, made a mud pie, and packed it on the man's eyes. As we know from other scriptural accounts of His miracles, Jesus could have simply spoken healing to the blind man. He could have healed him with a touch. Jesus could have, but here He chose to work through soil. Why? Perhaps because of the question the disciples asked of Him when they approached. The question is very important as we uncover the rich meaning of the ground and soil.

- The disciples asked, "Rabbi, who sinned, this man or his parents, that he was born blind?" (John 9:2). They saw blindness and immediately associated it with punishment for sin. Jesus didn't get angry with His disciples for asking this. He answered, "It was not that this man sinned, or his parents, but that the works of God might be displayed in him." John 9:3

The ripper blade cuts five feet into the ground, preparing the way for grapevine roots.

This is the question of our day too! "Jesus, a child died. You could have healed him. Who are You punishing?" "Jesus, my friend had cancer. You could have healed her. Who are You punishing? Her parents? Her daughter?" Jesus doesn't get angry at our asking. He answers, "It was not that this person sinned, but that the works of God might be displayed."

We want to attach illness, pain, and suffering to God's punishment for sin and wrath toward evil. Jesus calls us to a deeper understanding. The Word of God is clear: God punished Adam and Eve with death, which He would not have done had they obeyed. The punishment was for their disobedience, and we are inheritors. The Scriptures are clear! Jesus took our punishment—Adam's sin and our sin—in His body to the cross as payment for the punishment God placed on Adam. Christ passed through the soil, through the ground, and brought life.

God welcomes our "why" questions; God welcomes our cries; God welcomes our anger and our pain. He holds us and gently invites us to grow and embrace His Word as He works in us and through us. He invites us to receive just as He invited the blind man to receive the saliva and soil and the instructions to go and wash. In effect, Jesus says, "It was not that you sinned, but that the works of God might be displayed in you."

The religious leaders were completely confounded by the events, confounded by mud and the instructions to go wash, confounded by a blind man being healed on the Sabbath Day. John dedicated an entire chapter of his book to communicating what he desperately wants us to learn here. John concludes chapter 9 with Jesus revealing Himself to the blind man, who didn't even know who Jesus was but received His work through the soil nevertheless. John also reveals the hearts of the religious leaders (rocky or thorn-filled soil), which were further hardened as Jesus revealed Himself. The soil of the heart of the blind man was fertile and ready to receive:

> Jesus heard that they [religious leaders] had cast him out, and having found him [the healed man] He said, "Do you believe in the Son of Man?" He answered, "And who is He, sir, that I may believe in Him?" Jesus said to him, "You have seen Him, and it is He who is speaking to you." He said, "Lord, I believe," and he worshiped Him. John 9:35–38

The blind man met the Son of Man in the mud, saliva, and word, yet Jesus says, "You have seen Him, and it is He who is speaking to you." How was this possible? Did the blind man "see" Jesus even before he was healed? Yes! The soil of his heart bore the fruit of seeing, the fruit of faith. He saw and received Jesus' work with his heart without seeing with his eyes.

What are our blind spots? What keeps us from "seeing" Jesus' work for us and in us? Do we prefer to avoid messy interactions with Jesus? In this particular account, Jesus' work was not sanitary or done at an arm's length; it was messy and up close. It involved spit and soil; it involved placing mud on the man's eyes. Receiving from Jesus according to the way in which He wants to give means receiving by faith. Jesus' work isn't neat or tidy or sanitary!

Disking smooths the soil in preparation
for planting the vineyard.

The soil calls us to see Jesus with eyes of faith that are wide open to His past and present work. The soil of the ground calls us to ponder Adam's name, which means ground. Adam, taken from the ground, was the crown of creation. The soil teaches us the gravity of Adam's disobedience and its impact on our daily lives. The ground teaches us that the second Adam, Christ, God incarnate, took on human flesh to redeem us from the mess created by the first Adam's disobedience, from our sin and from the mess of our own disobedience.

Receiving Jesus' Word and work for us and in us without messiness would be like me trying to farm veggies or grapes without getting dirty. We want to keep Christ in a sterile environment, just like Peter wanted when he told Jesus that He should not face the cross. We want to keep ourselves in a sterile environment, but life doesn't happen that way. The blind man didn't say, "Saliva and mud? Yuck, no way! I'll just stay blind, thank you very much." He received and was healed.

The soil of the heart of the blind man was fertile, so the seed of the Word of God took root quickly. He, an uneducated man, spoke the Word of God to the religious leaders. "So for the second time they called the man who had been blind and said to him, 'Give glory to God. We know that this man [Jesus] is a sinner.' He answered, 'Whether He is a sinner I do not know. One thing I do know, that though I was blind, now I see'" (John 9:24–25).

The blind man's life didn't become easier after the seed of the Word took hold. He was questioned by the religious leaders, accused of blindness as a result of horrible sin, and thrown out of his place of worship. He was ridiculed because he didn't know who had healed him.

The soil of the hearts of the religious leaders was revealed through their words and actions toward the man and Jesus. They were religious leaders; therefore, they believed they were doing God's work. They would have nothing to do with Jesus' work through common soil or with a blind man whose simple words cut to the quick. They would not receive Jesus, honor Him, or allow the seed of His Word to grow in their hearts.

Journeying deeper into the Word of God calls us deeper into the soil of our hearts. The cry of our hearts becomes, "Jesus, guide us, teach us, cultivate us, and heal our blindness." Our cry becomes, "Jesus, work through whatever means necessary to bring growth of Your seed in the soil of our hearts. If it is joy and beauty, work through it; if it is healthy relationships, work through them; if it is ending unhealthy relationships, work through it; if it is illness, work through it; if it is dying and death, work through it; if it is tragedy, work through it." The soil of the ground teaches us to trust Jesus at His word of mercy, His healing, and His call to grow.

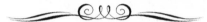

For individual study, meditate on the following questions and additional verses. For small-group study, discuss these questions:

1. What has the ground and soil revealed to you through these pages? What additional thoughts or Scripture verses came to mind and heart as you meditated on your calling? What temptation do you face that would draw you outside your calling?

2. Plant seeds in soil. Watch them grow. As they grow, imagine God at work in the soil of your heart and His Word as the seed sprouting and growing. What did you learn about yourself through the process? What can you learn about mercy and love by watching a seed grow?

3. Read and meditate on John 9. John wrote just twenty-one chapters, yet dedicated an entire chapter to this one story. What more can we learn about the soil of the ground? What can we learn about Jesus, the Word of God?

Chapter Four

STONE

All stones are rocks, and as our journey into the Scriptures through *The Rock Speaks* continues, we contemplate stones. Precious and semiprecious stones abound. I've heard it said that "a stone is a rock someone is willing to pay for." Experts have categorized hundreds of unique stones, many of which are found only in specific regions of the world, and many types of stones are used extensively in construction and decoration.

The famous Rosetta Stone, a large piece of black granite, is on display in the British Museum. It was inscribed in 196 BC with an edict by King Ptolemy V. After it was rediscovered in 1799, scholars began working to decode it. Unlocking the hieroglyphic inscription, which had been written in three languages, opened a window into ancient history. The term Rosetta Stone has come to be associated with "decrypting encoded information."

Alabaster, basalt, bluestone, granite, slate, limestone, marble, travertine, soapstone, quartzite, and onyx are categories of stone used in construction, both heavy and delicate. These stones are used for floors, columns, dishware, and jars. Around the world, unique stones are mined within each category. For example, deposits of alabaster are found in England, Belgium, India, Turkey, Cyprus, the United States, Italy, and Spain. Onyx had been mined in Egypt and is now mined primarily in Brazil. Beautiful alabaster jars from as early as 3500 BC are on display in British museums, and carvings from onyx date back to the days of Christ.

The Tomb of the Unknown Soldier at Arlington National Cemetery in Virginia is made of Yule marble, which is mined in Colorado. The Lincoln Memorial is crafted of beautiful granite, limestone, and marble, mined in both the North and the South, from Massachusetts, Colorado, Tennessee, Alabama, and Georgia. These stones were intentionally chosen from these regions by the craftsmen to reflect Abraham Lincoln's successful efforts to unite the states.

The most fascinating granite I have ever seen is Half Dome in California's Yosemite National Park. Half Dome rises nearly 5,000 feet above the valley floor to an elevation of more than 8,800 feet above sea level. My friends and I started our day hike from the valley floor at 4 a.m. on September 11, 2010. Headlamps provided the only light at first, but the light of the sun dawned on the new day as, step by step, we made our trek toward the granite slab. Seeing Half Dome from the valley floor is stunning. Seeing Half Dome up close is breathtaking. And knowing I was climbing to the top was truly exhilarating!

The clear blue sky was the perfect backdrop. I had prepared for the climb, but nothing prepared me for the breathtaking sights I saw and the absolute adrenaline rush I felt at the bottom of "the cables." The cables were set into the stone in the 1940s. They are far enough apart for only one person at a time, yet people were passing in both directions. Therefore, I was reminded of the fact that getting to the top also meant climbing back down . . . and so I watched with great intensity.

While scaling the intense vertical climb, it is necessary to pay close attention to the people in front of you on the cables. What if they fall? Not a good thought! And close attention to the people climbing down is also necessary, as both climbers need to turn sideways to grasp only one of the two cables. I considered the facts I had learned in preparation for the climb. People die climbing Half Dome! I quickly assured myself that they die by lightning strikes or by falling from slippery granite due to rain. (The sky was clear.) People also fall to their death because they try to race their way to the top or back down by traveling outside the cables. (I was not going to do that!)

Using the cables to descend the very steep granite of Half Dome, Yosemite National Park, California.

Climbing up was extremely challenging, but our group pressed on. Our goal was to make it to the top, almost a mile above the valley floor, and we made it safely. After cheering with my friends, I sat down for a snack, took off my shoes, and dangled my feet over the edge. The photos capture only a fraction of the beauty from the top of that grand piece of granite.

Then we set off to hike the nine miles back down to our starting point. We scaled safely down the monstrous stone using the cables, pausing only to take photos. Grueling! Our legs were weary and our feet not so steady on the slippery granite and steep decline. We learned that we should have set another really important goal: "To make it back to the car!" The shirt I purchased at the bottom read, "I made it to the top." It could have more accurately read, "I made it to the top and back!"

My Half Dome experiences have helped to shape my way of thinking about passing through fear, weariness, and pain in order to grow. Stones are part of something big, and they remind us that we are part of something bigger. Use the brief list following to think about their many uses, and then add to the list:

- We wear stones as jewelry.

- We enjoy art carved from stone.

- We use granite or marble countertops in our homes.

- We marvel at stones on display in museums.

- We stand in awe at stones God displays in nature.

- Stones were used throughout the Scriptures to reveal God's heart of mercy as well as God's demand for perfect justice.

- The Rock speaks through stones in this chapter to draw us into a deeper relationship with Him.

STONING

Stone is a noun. *Stoning* is a verb, an action word meaning "killing with stones." Stoning someone to death by hurling rocks at them is unimaginable to me. Death by stoning surely didn't happen quickly. It would have been slow and painful and extremely ugly.

We know from modern baseball that if a ball, thrown hard enough, strikes someone in the temple, it could kill the person instantly. A fast-moving ball striking the body anywhere else can cause bruises, concussion, or broken bones. Imagining stoning is not a pleasant exercise! We won't spend a lot of time on the subject, but it is important for our study.

We imagine stoning as in the epic David and Goliath story where David, a master slingman, chose five smooth stones from the riverbed. He placed one stone in his sling, the sling went round and round (like the little song), the rock flew, hit Goliath in the forehead, and killed him instantly (1 Samuel 17). One stone and instant death by stoning. That is somewhat palatable and a great story of God working through David to rescue a captive people.

There are many other stories in Scripture that are not easily digested. Scripture says that Cain rose up against his brother in the field and killed him. Cain was a farmer and perhaps used a stone to kill Abel (Genesis 4). Ahab and his evil wife, Jezebel, plotted against Naboth, a humble vineyard owner. Ahab wanted the vineyard, so he and his wife had witnesses testify falsely that Naboth had blasphemed God. Naboth was stoned to death, and Ahab took possession of the vineyard (1 Kings 21).

Wickedness raged in the hearts of people, and at times, that evil, through cold calculation or violent rage, was expressed by stoning. While we may not be able to visualize death by stoning, we can comprehend coldness and rage because we see it in our modern world—maybe not in stoning, but certainly in other forms of murder. Murder isn't something new, although the means through which it takes place are new in recent generations.

Digging further into the Scriptures challenges our hearts even more with this hard reality: God demands perfect justice. God commanded the taking of life by stoning to fulfill His demand. Here are a few examples of God's demand.

- God commanded that anyone who blasphemed the name of the Lord be put to death by stoning at the hands of the people of the camp:

  Whoever blasphemes the name of the LORD shall surely be put to death. All the congregation shall stone him. The sojourner as well as the native, when he blasphemes the Name, shall be put to death. Leviticus 24:16

- God commanded that a prophet or dreamer who draws people away from the one true God be stoned:

  If your brother, the son of your mother, or your son or your daughter or the wife you embrace or your friend who is as your own soul entices you secretly, saying, 'Let us go and serve other gods,' which neither you nor your fathers have known, some of the gods of the peoples who are around you, whether near you or far off from you, from the one end of the earth to the other, you shall not yield to him or listen to him, nor shall your eye pity him, nor shall you spare him, nor shall you conceal him. But you shall kill him. Your hand shall be first against him to put him to death, and afterward the hand of all the people. You shall stone him to death with stones, because he sought to draw you away from the LORD your God, who brought you out of the land of Egypt, out of the house of slavery. Deuteronomy 13:6–10

- A man who gathered sticks on the Sabbath Day was to be put to death by stoning, according to God's command, as punishment for breaking the Sabbath:

While the people of Israel were in the wilderness, they found a man gathering sticks on the Sabbath day. And those who found him gathering sticks brought him to Moses and Aaron and to all the congregation. They put him in custody, because it had not been made clear what should be done to him. And the LORD said to Moses, "The man shall be put to death; all the congregation shall stone him with stones outside the camp." And all the congregation brought him outside the camp and stoned him to death with stones, as the Lord commanded Moses. Numbers 15:32–36

God's demand and command are beyond our realm of human understanding—unimaginable, like stoning someone to death. His demand for perfection is unwavering. His demand is real; it is hard. Scripture doesn't allow us to ignore His demand and command. Scripture doesn't allow us to set it aside and talk about stones and stoning in a removed and sterile way. We wrestle with the Word of God, and we must dig a little deeper as we reflect on stones in our study.

WRITTEN ON STONE

God brought the people of Israel out of hard slavery in Egypt. The desert should have taken only weeks to cross, but it was the home of the wandering Israelites for two generations. God's deliverance from slavery became forty years of wandering because of the people's stubborn disobedience. God fed them from heaven, provided water out of a rock, gave them clothes and sandals that never wore out. Forty years in the desert gave the children of Israel many opportunities to obey God and many opportunities to work against Him.

God called Moses up to Mount Sinai for an important conversation that resulted in the Commandments (Exodus 31–34), which God wrote on stone tablets: "And He gave to Moses, when He had finished speaking with him on Mount Sinai, the two tablets of the testimony, tablets of stone, written with the finger of God" (Exodus 31:18).

God wrote His holy desire for His chosen people on tablets of stone with His finger. That intentional act was an act of mercy, a gift. Moses carried those stones to the bottom of the mountain, but rather than presenting God's gift to the people, he threw the stones to the ground in anger. The people, with the help of Aaron, Moses' right-hand man, had built a golden calf, an idol to worship. Moses ground up the gold and made the people drink it.

Moses went up the mountain a second time to talk with God. Moses cut a stone, per God's instructions, and carried it up the mountain. Then, for a second time, God wrote the Commandments for Moses and the people on the stone. Scripture says:

> Then Moses turned and went down from the mountain with the two tablets of the testimony in his hand, tablets that were written on both sides; on the front and on the back they were written. The tablets were the work of God, and the writing was the writing of God, engraved on the tablets. Exodus 32:15–16

The Ten Commandments were written on stone twice by the hand of God. The stone tablets were the work of God. They were given to a free people, a people who had been delivered from slavery. Those stone tablets and the words written on them by the finger of God were *never* intended to make slaves of free people. The people of God had already been delivered from slavery at great cost. A loving God would never drive them into a different slavery through His words.

The Ten Commandments were also *never* intended to make free a people who already had been freed. The Commandments were and are God's work to reveal His heart and desire, as well as His demand and command, for people to live lives of freedom. Just as Adam keeping God's one command would have been an act of worship, free people live in relationship with and in true worship of a holy God who has accomplished deliverance for them and in them.

Misunderstanding God's demand for holiness and His work through the stone tablets, through the Ten Commandments, leads to hearts of stone. Again, God does not make slaves through the Ten Commandments, nor does He free people through them. The Commandments create structure for living in relationship to God and to other people. The "don'ts" and the "dos" show us God's holy command and demand; the "shall nots" and the "shalls" guide us in daily living in relationship with our Creator and with our neighbors.

Row 124, the leaving place.

"Thou shall have no other Gods before Me," such as money, power, or fame, teaches us that the one true God is a jealous God. "Thou shall not take God's name in vain" through blasphemy or swear words teaches us that God's name, YAHWEH, is holy. "Thou shall not kill" with a stone or a bullet or poison teaches us that life is precious to God. "Thou shall not commit adultery" by thought or deed teaches us that marriage is precious to God. These were serious commands with serious consequences, such as death by stoning.

Jesus took the Ten Commandments and the subsequent laws God laid down for the Israelites seriously, far more seriously than the religious leaders of the day. Jesus did not water down the holiness of God or the demand of His perfect, righteous Father, the giver of the commands. Here are Christ's words from the Sermon on the Mount:

> Do not think that I have come to abolish the Law or the Prophets; I have not come to abolish them but to fulfill them. For truly, I say to you, until heaven and earth pass away, not an iota, not a dot, will pass from the Law until all is accomplished. Therefore whoever relaxes one of the least of these commandments and teaches others to do the same will be called least in the kingdom of heaven, but whoever does them and teaches them will be called great in the kingdom of heaven. For I tell you, unless your righteousness exceeds that of the scribes and Pharisees, you will never enter the kingdom of heaven. Matthew 5:17–20

> You therefore must be perfect, as your heavenly Father is perfect. Matthew 5:48

We are called to take the Law of God seriously, to live by the Law, always recognizing and believing that it does not enslave us. We are called to take God's Law seriously, to live by it, always recognizing and believing that it does not free us. Christ has freed us—completely. We are called to trust God at His word of mercy, the word that abundantly proclaims, "My Son has accomplished My demand for perfection perfectly for you." We are children of the promise because Christ fulfilled the Law perfectly.

STONES TO THROW AT HIM

God commanded that stones be used to take the life of individuals who blasphemed Him, dreamers who drew people away from the one true God, and those who worked on the Sabbath Day. We know Jesus took the Law seriously, but according to the religious leaders, He fit this Old Testament description of a lawbreaker, of one God commanded be stoned! The religious leaders believed they were doing their job when they picked up stones to stone Jesus.

> [Jesus said,] "Your father Abraham rejoiced that he would see My day. He saw it and was glad." So the Jews said to Him, "You are not yet fifty years old, and have You seen Abraham?" Jesus said to them, "Truly, truly, I say to you, before Abraham was, I am." So they picked up stones to throw at Him, but Jesus hid Himself and went out of the temple. John 8:56–59

> [Jesus said,] "My Father, who has given them to Me, is greater than all, and no one is able to snatch them out of the Father's hand. I and the Father are one." The Jews picked up stones again to stone Him. Jesus answered them, "I have shown you many good works from the Father; for which of them are you going to stone Me?" The Jews answered Him, "It is not for a good work that we are going to stone You but for blasphemy, because You, being a man, make Yourself God." John 10:29–33

And this was why the Jews were persecuting Jesus, because He was doing these things on the Sabbath. But Jesus answered them, "My Father is working until now, and I am working." This was why the Jews were seeking all the more to kill Him, because not only was He breaking the Sabbath, but He was even calling God His own Father, making Himself equal with God. John 5:16–18

The religious leaders believed they were doing the work of God. And they were, if the sentence of stoning was examined by the letter of the Law. But they failed to trust the promises of God through the Good News of mercy in Christ. Jesus proclaimed Himself Messiah, the fulfillment of all of God's promises, yet their hearts were hard. Rather than being free to receive Him, their stone hearts were focused on protecting God from His own Son!

The Ten Commandments and the subsequent laws that God demanded the people of Israel live by were strict. As we have said, these laws were not given to enslave or free a delivered people. Christ Jesus was and is the fulfillment of God's holy demand and command. Christ is the righteous one, the promised one on whom all of the demands of God and the promises of God rested then and rest now for us. Stephen, the first New Testament believer who was killed for his faith and confession, was stoned to death. He spoke these words to the religious leaders:

"You stiff-necked people, uncircumcised in heart and ears, you always resist the Holy Spirit. As your fathers did, so do you. Which of the prophets did your fathers not persecute? And they killed those who announced beforehand the coming of the Righteous One, whom you have now betrayed and murdered, you who received the law as delivered by angels and did not keep it." Now when they heard these things they were enraged, and they ground their teeth at him. But he, full of the Holy Spirit, gazed into heaven and saw the glory of God, and Jesus standing at the right hand of God. And he said, "Behold, I see the heavens opened, and the Son of Man standing at the right hand of God." But they cried out with a loud voice and stopped their ears and rushed together at him. Then they cast him out of the city and stoned him. Acts 7:51–58

We know Stephen as the man whose words God worked through to call Saul to faith in Christ. Stephen was cast out of the city and stoned for blasphemy. The religious leaders and their fathers were so bound in the laws of God that they could not see the promises of God in the prophets or the mercy of God in Christ. Blinded, the religious leaders would not receive Jesus as the Messiah, could not receive His mercy or show mercy to others. Just as their fathers had done, they killed by stoning the bearers of the words of Law and mercy.

At the time of the Early Church, hearts of stone became harder with misunderstanding and misinterpretation of the laws of God and the mercy of God. The same is true today. Yet hearts of flesh that are transformed by the Spirit become more loving, gentle, and merciful as they receive mercy from the One who fulfilled all righteousness.

Hearts of Stone; Hearts of Flesh

The profound imagery of "a heart of stone" and "a heart of flesh" reveals God's heart and God's way. We inherited "hearts of stone" through Adam's disobedience. We needed a heart transplant; the Great Physician performed an operation. He replaced our heart of stone with a heart of flesh, through the call to faith, through Holy Baptism, by grafting us into the life of Christ. Our hearts of flesh are alive, beating with gratitude and mercy.

The prophet Ezekiel provided rich words on which to meditate, using the imagery of "a heart of stone" and "a heart of flesh":

> And I will give them one heart, and a new spirit I will put within them. I will remove the heart of stone from their flesh and give them a heart of flesh, that they may walk in My statutes and keep My rules and obey them. And they shall be My people, and I will be their God. Ezekiel 11:19–20 (See also 36:23–28.)

The Word and work of God removes the heart of stone and places within us hearts of flesh. As we grow in faith, we grow in understanding, love, and mercy from the heart.

The minds of the religious leaders were sharp. They knew the laws, and they picked up stones to stone Jesus and Lazarus and Stephen. They didn't have hearts of flesh. Their hearts of stone became even harder as they witnessed the seed of the Word of God grow in the soil of fertile hearts of flesh. Jealousy, rage, and hatred were the products of their hearts of stone.

The more Jesus spoke mercy into people's lives, healed the sick, and raised the dead, the more unseeing and hard-hearted the religious leaders became. Eventually, they became stone-hard as they plotted to kill the Christ. Christ spoke harshly to those with stone hearts and tenderly to those with hearts of flesh.

Saul was present at the stoning of Stephen. His heart was hard, and he was zealous to cleanse the world of those who followed Christ, who Saul believed to be a Sabbath-breaking blasphemer. His spiritual blindness was interrupted by a blinding light and the words of the Christ. He experienced a heart transplant and a name change. We know him as the apostle Paul, who spoke and wrote the true understanding of the Ten Commandments and the mercy of a perfect God.

Hard hearts abound today too. Many of today's religious leaders confuse exactly the same issues by confusing the laws of God and the promises of God. Unfortunately, the law of God is spoken harshly to people with tender hearts of flesh; the mercy of God is spoken into hearts of stone. Perhaps we have heard only stone-cold words when we needed warm words of mercy. We may struggle with hearing and taking to heart words of mercy because we picture only a God who is ready to stone us. This leads to horrible confusion and a hurting Body of Christ. Jesus spoke mercy and love to the broken, to those who looked to Him in faith. The Gospels and letters to the churches in the New Testament are clear. Christ fulfilled the Law perfectly in our place; He gives us a heart transplant and gives us life and breath through His Spirit. His life breeds life, and our lives are a living testament to His life in us.

The apostle Paul speaks the truth this way to the Jesus followers in Corinth: "You yourselves are our letter of recommendation, written on our hearts, to be known and read by all. And you show that you are a letter from Christ delivered by us, written not with ink but with the Spirit of the living God, not on tablets of stone but on tablets of human hearts" (2 Corinthians 3:2–3). Jesus and the apostles spoke harsh words, but only as a wake-up call to the stone-cold, the hard-hearted. Some words were received into transplanted hearts; some hearts rejected the words and became hardened to Christ's love and mercy.

God's harsh words through the prophets in the Old Testament were a call to turn from unbelief to faith in the living God. Zechariah said, "They made their hearts diamond-hard lest they should hear the law and the words that the LORD of hosts had sent by His Spirit through the former prophets" (Zechariah 7:12).

For many, words of command, demand, and punishment are easy to hear and take because it may be all we've known. We've been trained to wait for God to "throw the first stone." We reason, "God was angry at the people for their disobedience, so He must be angry at us." Like the disciples and religious leaders, when something bad happens, we ask, "Who sinned?" Like those before us, we ask, "What did I do wrong to deserve this?"

Jesus gently calls us to hear the words of the promise, which are more challenging to hear and receive, to grasp and hold. Jesus said, "Neither this man or his parents sinned, but he is blind so that My work might be revealed in him." God's promises were fulfilled in Christ, as were God's commands and demands. We are called to trust, to allow His Word to soften our hearts to His Word and work; we are called to receive His Word and work in us; we are called to be merciful to ourselves; we are called to be merciful to others.

TAKE AWAY THE STONE

The story of Lazarus is for us! Jesus was not there when His friend died. Mary and Martha were upset and sad. Martha said, "Lord, if You had been here, my brother would not have died. But even now I know that whatever You ask from God, God will give You" (John 11:21–22). Here is their conversation:

> Jesus said to her, "Your brother will rise again." Martha said to Him, "I know that he will rise again in the resurrection on the last day." Jesus said to her, "I am the resurrection and the life. Whoever believes in Me, though he die, yet shall he live, and everyone who lives and believes in Me shall never die. Do you believe this?" She said to Him, "Yes, Lord; I believe that You are the Christ, the Son of God, who is coming into the world." John 11:23–27

We pray for strength and
courage as we learn to cast
our cares upon Him.

Martha believed; Mary believed. We believe too. Martha's testimony is a testament of faith in Christ; her words are beautiful. Much is revealed in the next verses. Their faith and confession was strong until Jesus asked them to do the unexpected:

Then Jesus, deeply moved again, came to the tomb. It was a cave, and a stone lay against it. Jesus said, "Take away the stone." Martha, the sister of the dead man, said to Him,

> "Lord, by this time there will be an odor, for he has been dead four days." Jesus said to her, "Did I not tell you that if you believed you would see the glory of God?" So they took away the stone. John 11:38–41

Martha and Mary were in shock. Their brother had been buried four days earlier. They were sad and angry too, because Jesus hadn't been there. Martha didn't lack faith when she stated the obvious, that her brother's body would stink of death. Her reasoning was sound. Jesus called Martha and Mary beyond reason to trust in Him as THE resurrection and THE life.

Stones remind us; they teach us to go beyond reason to trust as we live life in Christ. We believe that Christ is the resurrection and that one day we will rise. Stones remind us and teach us that Christ says "Take away the stone" to us. Our hearts of flesh embrace His words and heed the call. The grave of fear, challenge, illness, or pain cannot hold us because His call to "come forth" is for us, now. We say, "Jesus, this _____ stinks." Jesus says, "Take away the stone!" Jesus says, "Let My work, work. Let My glory shine through this circumstance. Go beyond reason and trust Me as the resurrection and the life for you."

Stones remind us and teach us to trust that Jesus' tomb, cut from stone, with a large stone rolled to cover the entrance, did not hold Him.

> On the first day of the week, at early dawn, they went to the tomb, taking the spices they had prepared. And they found the stone rolled away from the tomb, but when they went in they did not find the body of the Lord Jesus. While they were perplexed about this, behold, two men stood by them in dazzling apparel. And as they were frightened and bowed their faces to the ground, the men said to them, "Why do you seek the living among the dead?" Luke 24:1–5

The stone grave was the *only* place Jesus promised that He would *not* be, yet the grave was the only place the women and the disciples looked for Him. The disciples and the women were shocked and dismayed. Their minds were closed to the possibilities. Stones teach us to look for life where Christ promises life will be! Life is not *in* the stone tomb; life is *through* the tomb, both today and for eternity.

For individual study, meditate on the following questions. For small-group study, discuss these questions:

1. What have stones revealed to you through these pages? What additional thoughts or Scripture verses came to your mind and heart as you meditated on these words?

2. Think about why it is so easy to believe that the Law of God makes us slaves or, at the other extreme, makes us free.

3. Christ fulfilled the Law perfectly in our place. How does that free us to live?

CHRISTI CRUX EST MIHI LUX

CORNERSTONE OF FIRST CONCORDIA BUILDING
1907 – 46

IN THANKSGIVING TO GOD FOR OUR NORTHWEST
LUTHERAN FOREBEARS AND IN PRAYERFUL ASSURANCE
OF GREATER KINGDOM ACCOMPLISHMENT IN THE FUTURE

PRESENTED BY
THE LUTHERAN LAYMEN'S LEAGUE

APRIL 15, 1961

Chapter Five

Cornerstone and Keystone

Cornerstones and keystones are very specialized stones, used for specific purposes, and so we reflect on them as we continue into *The Rock Speaks*.

Ancient structures and ruins give us examples of how these stones were used. The cornerstone of a building was the most important piece of the foundation. A large square or rectangular stone, it was placed first in the construction of the building and was the stone upon which all other stones were set. The cornerstone was often carved with the date construction began.

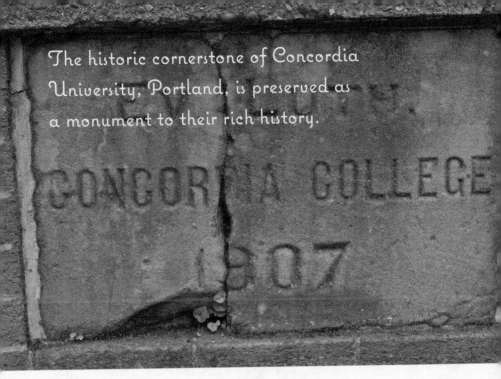

The historic cornerstone of Concordia University, Portland, is preserved as a monument to their rich history.

By contrast, the keystone was the final stone placed in the top center of an arched entryway. Wedge-shaped and sized precisely to fit into the opening, the keystone was often carved with art reflecting the structure's purpose. *Capstone* is often used synonymously with *keystone*.

Both keystones and cornerstones were placed ceremoniously.

Modern architecture might integrate these historic features into buildings, but this is done for aesthetics and not by necessity, as in the past. Ceremonies are common with the laying of the cornerstone, which might have a space cut into the side where mementos or artifacts are placed and then covered by an engraved plate—a time capsule, in other words. At a major anniversary, that time capsule might be opened and those items revisited as part of the celebration. Keystones, decorated with the theme of the building, are still often placed with ceremony as well, as the building is commissioned at a grand opening.

Cornerstone and *keystone* are common words in modern language. *Cornerstone* means "the foundation upon which something is built";

keystone means "the piece that holds all pieces in place." We might reflect, "The cornerstone of a free nation is freedom of speech." Or, "The keystone of health is proper diet, exercise, and rest." Churches, universities, and businesses use *cornerstone, keystone,* and *capstone* in their names. A quick Internet search of "Cornerstone Church" provides millions of results. The same is true of "keystone businesses," "capstone university curriculum," and so forth. Military and leadership companies have "capstone programs." Foundational integrity seems to be the common theme conveyed by using these words in this way.

The Scriptures reveal Christ as the cornerstone, the stone upon which all other stones are placed. The Scriptures also reveal Christ as the keystone, the final stone of the building. As we continue into *The Rock Speaks,* we meditate on Christ, the first stone and the last stone, the Alpha and Omega; Christ the foundation stone and the finishing stone. The themes and verses we will explore in this chapter provide evidence for us, as they have through the ages, that the Christ is the cornerstone foretold by the Scriptures and fulfilled by His life, death, and resurrection.

CHRIST THE CORNERSTONE

The words of Christ "The stone that the builders rejected has become the cornerstone" are recorded by Matthew, Mark, and Luke. Jesus was talking about Himself to a large audience made up of disciples and religious leaders. His question to the religious leaders preceding His revelation as the fulfillment of Psalm 118:22–23 and Isaiah 28:16 is important.

- Jesus said to them, **"Have you never read in the Scriptures:** 'The stone that the builders rejected has become the cornerstone; this was the Lord's doing, and it is marvelous in our eyes'?" Matthew 21:42 (emphasis added)

- **"Have you not read this Scripture:** 'The stone that the builders rejected has become the cornerstone; this was the Lord's doing, and it is marvelous in our eyes'?" Mark 12:10–11 (emphasis added)

- But He looked directly at them and said, **"What then is this that is written:** 'The stone that the builders rejected has become the cornerstone'?" Luke 20:17 (emphasis added)

"Have you never read in the Scriptures?" was Jesus' question, directed to the most highly educated people in Jewish society, the religious elite who knew the Scriptures, who translated the Scriptures, who taught the Scriptures. The elite were trying to trap Jesus with their questions in order to get rid of the carpenter from Nazareth who was causing a religious movement, a rebellion from the traditions of the Law. Jesus was leading people to faith in Himself and away from religion.

The crowd listening to this interaction most likely included blue-collar workers, who may have understood Jesus' message because of their hands-on experience with construction. The religious leaders, on the other hand, were white-collar men who did not know the building trade. To say that the "builders rejected" a "cornerstone" implied that they didn't know their trade and, worse yet, were unskilled and inept.

Rather than trap Jesus with their questions, the opposite happened. It was the religious leaders who were trapped and silenced. Matthew, Mark, and Luke record that the religious leaders no longer dared ask any more questions and they feared the crowds. Their determination to thwart Jesus' ministry was fueled by religious furry. Their blindness and hardness of heart kept them from "seeing" Jesus in these Old Testament passages.

Jesus' question flowed directly into the revelation: "I am the cornerstone which the builders rejected. The Scriptures you believe you know so well were talking about Me. You, the builders, are rejecting Me." Contrast this with Luke's early record of Jesus proclaiming Himself the fulfillment of the Scriptures as He spoke in the synagogue:

The scroll of the prophet Isaiah was given to Him. He unrolled the scroll and found the place where it was written, "The Spirit of the LORD is upon Me, because He has anointed Me to proclaim good news to the poor. He has sent Me to proclaim liberty to the captives and recovering of sight to the blind, to set at liberty those who are oppressed, to proclaim the year of the Lord's favor." And He rolled up the scroll and gave it back to the attendant and sat down. And the eyes of all in the synagogue were fixed on Him. And He began to say to them, "Today this Scripture has been fulfilled in your hearing." And **all spoke well of Him and marveled at the gracious words that were coming from His mouth.** And they said, "Is not this Joseph's son?" Luke 4:17–22 (emphasis added)

All spoke well of Him *before* He worked His work and spoke the Word. The religious leaders' praise turned to murderous thoughts as His revelation of Himself as Messiah didn't match their expectations. They needed a Christ who would be just like them, not someone who would eat with sinners, forgive sins, work on the Sabbath, touch the unclean, and raise the dead. Jesus' next words cut deeply. "When the chief priests and the Pharisees heard His parables, they perceived that He was speaking about them. And although they were seeking to arrest Him, they feared the crowds, because they held Him to be a prophet" (Matthew 21:45–46).

The Pharisees, chief priests, and scribes were religious leaders, the holders of the Word of God. Yet they were filled with pride and arrogance. Their self-defined religion got in the way of seeing and hearing the Messiah, the long-awaited one, in their midst. Their religion hurt people, and this kind of religion still hurts people today. Self-defined religion is a barrier to true faith in Christ, to trusting Jesus at His word, and to an intimate relationship with the triune God. This kind of religion works to control God. Arguments about proper this or proper that, what the Church can and cannot do, can blind us to the Messiah's word and work.

Jesus comes to us and asks a simple, faith-based question: "What do you want Me to do for you?" Is the Christ, as He reveals Himself in the Scriptures, our cornerstone? Would Jesus say to us, "Have you never read the Scriptures?" The Cornerstone invites us to search the Scriptures, to be rooted, anchored, and built up in Him. Do we need to let go of anything that blinds us to Christ's word and work for us and in us? Is Christ our foundation? Would we have the courage of the blind men by the side of the road who begged Jesus for mercy more and more loudly despite the crowd that demanded silence (Matthew 20)?

Christ revealed Himself as the fulfillment of the Scriptures (Luke 4), as salvation to the household of Zacchaeus (Luke 19), and as the cornerstone. The apostles Paul and Peter quote Psalm 118 and Isaiah 28 as they reveal Jesus as the cornerstone and believers as the stones built upon the chief stone.

As we dig deeper, the word keystone, also called "capstone," deserves our attention. The cornerstone is the stone upon which all other stones are placed. The keystone is the final stone of the building.

CHRIST THE KEYSTONE

The Greek word for the "final stone" is used only twice in the New Testament, Ephesians 2:20 and 1 Peter 2:6. In both cases, the apostles reference Christ.[2] The Greek word for "final stone," *akrogōniaîos*, is translated "cornerstone" in many versions of the Scriptures. The Greek is clear;

---

2   *Theological Dictionary of the New Testament*, edited by Gerhard Kittel, Wm. B. Eerdmans Publishing Co., © 1964. Volume 1, p. 792; Volume 4, pp. 274–275.

Christ is the keystone, the final stone placed in the building that completes the structure.

The community of believers is the spiritual temple. Christ is the cornerstone; the apostles and prophets are the foundation; Christ is the keystone.

> So then you are no longer strangers and aliens, but you are fellow citizens with the saints and members of the household of God, built on the foundation of the apostles and prophets, Christ Jesus Himself being the [keystone], in whom the whole structure, being joined together, grows into a holy temple in the Lord. In Him you also are being built together into a dwelling place for God by the Spirit. Ephesians 2:19–22

The apostle Paul's imagery builds on Christ's proclamation of Himself as the fulfillment of the Old Testament promises that the Messiah would be the foundation and finishing stone of the building, the true temple. The true temple wasn't built by human hands; the builder is God, and we are being built together as stones in the true temple. We are begun and completed by the perfect Christ, which defines our worship of the true temple. Jesus' conversation with the woman at the well included this revelation:

> "The hour is coming, and is now here, when the true worshipers will worship the Father in spirit and truth, for the Father is seeking such people to worship Him. God is spirit, and those who worship Him must worship in spirit and truth." The woman said to Him, "I know that Messiah is coming (He who is called Christ). When He comes, He will tell us all things." Jesus said to her, "I who speak to you am He." John 4:23–26

Paul's words proclaimed a movement, by Christ's work and by the Spirit of the living God, away from the physical temple to Christ as the true temple. This reality was foreshadowed in the Scriptures. Christ spoke it when He responded to the Jews. "So the Jews said to Him, 'What sign do You show us for doing these things?' Jesus answered them, 'Destroy this temple, and in three days I will raise it up.' The Jews then said, 'It has taken forty-six years to build this temple, and will You raise it up in three days?' But He was speaking about the temple of His body" (John 2:18–21). The physical temple in Jerusalem would no longer serve as the dwelling place of God. Paul asked, "Do you not know that you are God's temple and that God's Spirit dwells in you?" (1 Corinthians 3:16).

Paul says that Christ is the keystone, the final stone, and we are fellow citizens in the temple of the Lord. We and all other stones of the holy temple of the Lord are the dwelling place for God by the Spirit. We are protected because Christ is cornerstone and keystone, beneath us and above us. We are citizens with all the saints, joined together by Christ in two magnificent ways.

We fit into this incredible picture of the stone the builders rejected because Christ has called us to be living stones in His building. We are citizens by His action, building us up in Him with all the saints. Our minds are easily drawn to the particular church building where we choose to worship, but Paul's image challenges us to so much more. The Church is the Body of Christ, the holy temple, a continual building project.

We are called to relinquish our human limitation of the work of the Master Designer and Builder. Following Christ means knowing the whole Scripture according to justice and mercy; following Christ means receiving the work He works for us and in us; following Christ means allowing His work to be alive through us as His hands and feet and voice in this world. The apostle Peter's imagery will help us unfold this further. Please carefully note that Peter begins by saying, "As you." You and I are the "you"!

> As you come to Him, a living stone rejected by men but in the sight of God chosen and precious, you yourselves like living stones are being built up as a spiritual house, to be a holy priesthood, to offer spiritual sacrifices acceptable to God through Jesus Christ. For it stands in Scripture: "Behold, I am laying in Zion a stone, a [keystone] chosen and precious, and whoever believes in Him will not be put to shame." So the honor is for you who believe, but for those who do not believe, "The stone that the builders rejected has become the cornerstone." 1 Peter 2:4–7

The building is made up of the Living Stone, Christ, and living stones—you, me, and all other believers. We are in fellowship with all other living stones—all the saints who have gone before us, all saints today, and all those who will follow. Living stones are being built up into a spiritual house, a constant project of the Master Builder, God.

The temple in Jerusalem was the spiritual house of the people of Israel. The curtain separating the people from the holiest place in the temple was torn in two when Jesus breathed His last breath as the final sacrifice. In that holiest place in the temple, the Jewish priesthood offered sacrifices on behalf of the people in the old covenant. Jesus was the final sacrifice, completing God's promises, which meant the curtain separating the people from the holiest place was obsolete. Today we offer spiritual sacrifices acceptable to God through faith in Christ. Peter declared that living stones are raised up to be the holy priesthood, to offer spiritual sacrifices acceptable to God through Jesus.

This was and is radical thinking, a profound call to believe and to trust that our lives as well as our praises are the spiritual sacrifice to the living

God. The author of Hebrews declared, "Through Him then let us continually offer up a sacrifice of praise to God, that is, the fruit of lips that acknowledge His name. Do not neglect to do good and to share what you have, for such sacrifices are pleasing to God" (Hebrews 13:15–16).

Think back to our discussion in chapter 3 of the blind man who received mud on his eyes, washed, and was healed (John 9). Jesus chose to touch the blind man's life and heal him. The religious leaders questioned the man relentlessly and finally threw him out of the temple. John said, "Jesus heard that they had cast him out, and having found him He said, 'Do you believe in the Son of Man?' He answered, 'And who is He, sir, that I may believe in Him?' Jesus said to him, 'You have seen Him, and it is He who is speaking to you.' He said, 'Lord, I believe,' and he worshiped Him'" (John 9:35–38).

As living stones of the Living Stone, we gather to be nourished and built up around the proclamation of the Word and the Supper of our Lord. We gather to offer praises and to pray together as the community of believers. And there is more! As living stones of the Living Stone, we offer continual praises with our very lives, trusting in His mercy, which builds us up in Him.

You, the Living Stones: Chosen, Precious

Can we possibly, truly trust Peter's words in these short verses? Can we comprehend his words, that we are living stones, being built up by Christ's Word and work? "As you come to Him, a living stone rejected by men but in the sight of God chosen and precious, you yourselves like living stones are being built up as a spiritual house, to be a holy priesthood, to offer spiritual sacrifices acceptable to God through Jesus Christ" (1 Peter 2:4–5).

Peter uses the image of us as a living stone of the Living Stone to draw us into a deeper understanding that we are chosen and precious. We are alive in Him because of His creation, His breath, and His sustenance. We are a significant piece of an incomprehensibly big, eternal building that is continuously crafted by God. That eternal picture reveals that the cornerstone of the Old Testament is the cornerstone and keystone of the New Testament. He created living stones of you and me, by His choosing, by His breath.

God chose to form Adam of dust, breathe life into that dust, and create a living being. God commanded Moses to strike a rock with his staff, and water flowed. John the Baptist declared, "And do not presume to say to yourselves, 'We have Abraham as our father,' for I tell you, God is able from these stones to raise up children for Abraham" (Matthew 3:9). To those who demanded silence of the cheering crowd in Jerusalem, Jesus said, "I tell you, if these were silent, the very stones would cry out" (Luke 19:40).

The living God chose to create life by His breath; the Living Stone chose to create living stones by His breath, Spirit, and Word. We are chosen, precious, holy, redeemed. Our aliveness flows from and through His life. Our spiritual sacrifices flow from our aliveness and the continual building that God works through His Word, His call.

What does a spiritual sacrifice look like? Make a list with me and join with me to celebrate being a living stone.

- Play and sing; laugh and cry; pray and praise; take care of your own body, soul, mind, heart, and spirit; take care of others and help them care for themselves; rejoice; grieve.

- Embrace fellowship with other living stones; meditate alone in the quiet.

- Reflect on the Scriptures; read, learn, and digest.

- Rejoice always, pray without ceasing, give thanks in all circumstances; for this is the will of God in Christ Jesus for you. Do not quench the Spirit. 1 Thessalonians 5:16–19

Note: Paul doesn't call us to give thanks *for* all circumstances, but *in* all circumstances.

- Finally, brothers [and sisters], whatever is true, whatever is honorable, whatever is just, whatever is pure, whatever is lovely, whatever is commendable, if there is any excellence, if there is anything worthy of praise, think about these things. Philippians 4:8

- Be merciful to me, O God, be merciful to me, for in You my soul takes refuge; in the shadow of Your wings I will take refuge, till the storms of destruction pass by. I cry out to God Most High, to God who fulfills His purpose for me. Psalm 57:1–2

- Receive the Word of God; embrace God's Word and work "for me"; speak the Word of God.

The beauty of being living stones is that not one living stone is exactly like another. The facets are as varied and unique as the gemstones of God's creation. The fruit of our lives flows from the Spirit of God living in us. Our calling is to live through our vocation, which is given by God and is precious to Him. God works through the messy, the challenging, the painful, and the joyful so that our light shines to reveal Him. God polishes us as living stones.

I'm drawn to the image of Christ's call to abide in Him through His words "I am the vine; you are the branches" (John 15:5). The tiny bud of the branch (us) is grafted into Christ, the Vine. The one-time process of grafting branches onto a rootstock that is not susceptible to disease and matches our soil and climate is the image of life "in" Christ.[3] Christ is holy, not susceptible to sin or death; we live in His life through the work of God, which has placed us in an intimate relationship with Him.

In the grafting process, the deep wound is made by the sharp knife and the tiny bud is placed into the cut. A Band-Aid-like substance holds the bud in place. A scab forms as healing begins. The scar that grows with the plant is a constant reminder of the wound, the healing, and the life that flows through the vine. Peter's words "by His wounds you are healed" come alive as we picture our lives, cut away from the old and placed into the life of Christ. He is our home, our dwelling place, our root. Christ, the Vine, is also the Living Stone, and we are living stones by His Word and work. This is a different image of the same Christ drawing us to life, fully in Him.

Peter knew the challenges of life, so among the verses we're digging into, he counsels, "Beloved, I urge you as sojourners and exiles [living stones] to abstain from the passions of the flesh, which wage war against your soul" (1 Peter 2:11). We, a perfectly free people, called to live holy lives within our vocation, often don't live as living stones. We enslave ourselves, looking for life where it cannot be found, a life and lifestyle that wages war against our soul. Recognizing, turning, and receiving mercy is the life to which God calls us, fully and completely, to live. Living stones of the Living Stone offer living sacrifices acceptable to God through expressing life fully and completely.

Stumbling Stone, a Stone That Crushes

Living stones are alive because of the breath and Spirit of the Living Stone. Living stones produce the fruit of the kingdom of God, as Jesus says in the following passage. As we conclude this chapter, we must dig into an

---

3   Steinbeck, Cindy. *The Vine Speaks* (St. Louis: Concordia Publishing House, 2013)

important—although challenging—aspect of Jesus, the cornerstone: He is the cornerstone . . . and a crushing stone.

> Jesus said to them, "Have you never read in the Scriptures: "'The stone that the builders rejected has become the cornerstone; this was the Lord's doing, and it is marvelous in our eyes'? Therefore I tell you, the kingdom of God will be taken away from you and given to a people producing its fruits. And **the one who falls on this stone will be broken to pieces; and when it falls on anyone, it will crush him."** When the chief priests and the Pharisees heard His parables, they perceived that He was speaking about them. And although they were seeking to arrest Him, they feared the crowds, because they held Him to be a prophet. Matthew 21:42–46 (emphasis added)
>
> Religious leaders thought they were producing the "fruit of God" as they tried to trap Jesus, whom they believed to be a blasphemer and Sabbath-breaker. They worked overtime among themselves to craft questions that would trap Jesus, and they watched His every move through their misguided understanding of religion. Their perception of Jesus' words was right—they were the "you" of whom Jesus spoke when He said, "the kingdom of God will be taken away from you and given to a people producing its fruits."[4]

Not only would the kingdom of God be taken away from religious leaders; but Jesus said the Living Stone, who gives life to those who receive Him, would crush those who reject Him. They rejected Jesus by following a set of strict rules, by enslaving others to those rules, and by hardening

---

4 For further study, reflect on Matthew 15:7–9: "You hypocrites! Well did Isaiah prophesy of you, when he said: "'This people honors Me with their lips, but their heart is far from Me; in vain do they worship Me, teaching as doctrines the commandments of men.'"

their hearts to mercy, both for themselves and others. The apostle Paul poses these questions:

> What shall we say, then? That Gentiles who did not pursue righteousness have attained it, that is, a righteousness that is by faith; but that Israel who pursued a law that would lead to righteousness did not succeed in reaching that law. Why? Because they did not pursue it by faith, but as if it were based on works. They have stumbled over the stumbling stone, as it is written, "Behold, I am laying in Zion a stone of stumbling, and a rock of offense; and whoever believes in Him will not be put to shame." Romans 9:30–33

The precious Cornerstone, who chooses stones and makes them alive, is also the Crushing Stone. Harsh? Yes. Hard to comprehend and embrace as the Word and will of God? Yes. Important to discern? Yes. God will not build the spiritual temple with stones that reject Him as the cornerstone and the keystone. As opposed to living stones that are being built up, hard-hearted stones will tumble, will be broken to pieces, and will be crushed by the Living Stone (Matthew 21:44).

Immediately after declaring God's promise of a cornerstone, Isaiah names the harsh reality of the work of God, His "alien" work (unknown, strange, peculiar, foreign): "For the LORD will rise up as on Mount Perazim; as in the Valley of Gibeon He will be roused; to do His deed—strange is His deed! and to work His work—alien is His work!" (Isaiah 28:21). God's perfect righteousness is His primary work; drawing people to Himself through His one and only perfect Son is His primary work. The work of judgment and justice is God's alien work. His alien work is fully necessary in order to be true to His perfect righteousness.

God declared through the prophet Ezekiel, "I have no pleasure in the death of the wicked, but that the wicked turn from his way and live"

(Ezekiel 33:11a). The Rock spoke to draw people from death to life; the Living Stone gave up His life, providing the way for all through His Father's grace and mercy, God's proper work. God's desire is that we learn the Scriptures, learn the truth of His mercy, love, and grace—His proper work. God's desire is that we learn the Scriptures, learn the truth of His justice—His alien work.

The promised Messiah, the righteousness of God in human skin, the one who lived life perfectly, bore our sin in His body and submitted Himself to God's alien work of perfect justice and judgment. He satisfied God's justice and demand for perfect righteousness in our place. Receiving His work by faith, not by works, gives full access to the primary work of God, the life-giving, life-building work of God. Receiving Christ's work frees us to live. We are free, living stones because of God's work and His Word.

The religious leaders were not free. With arrogance, lack of faith, and great zeal, they thought they were carrying out the proper work of God. Yet they perceived that Jesus was talking about them in His parables, and they were right. Rather than take a closer look at the Scriptures and the mercy with which Jesus ministered, they sought to silence Him once and for all. They stopped asking Jesus questions. They plotted in secret. Their murderous thoughts turned to action as they contracted with Judas to betray the Christ. They worked the political system to murder Jesus.

The gap between faith in the Messiah and rejection of the Messiah widened with every step Jesus took toward the cross. Many came to the Living Stone with humility and a desire to receive. They received God's proper work, His mercy, grace, and love. Many rejected Jesus and became more crafty, ugly, and murderous. They received God's alien work, Jesus' condemning words. Jesus could have removed Himself from their midst, but He chose the cross to take the punishment, God's alien work, on our behalf as the fulfillment of His earthly journey, the fulfillment of the Scriptures.

The Living Stone was crushed and the Crushing Stone was crushed by those who hung Him on the cross on Golgotha, the "skull" stone! By all outward appearances, those who rejected and murdered Jesus won. They got what they wanted, and rather than being crushed, they were successful. By all outward appearances, evil won on that Good Friday. Herein lies the challenge. We may see evil winning, illness winning, death winning. The Word of God comes to us and asks, Why do you seek Jesus in the alien work of God? "Why do you seek the living among the dead?" (Luke 24:5).

The only place people looked for Jesus after His crucifixion was the only place He promised He would not be. The stone was rolled away. The gravestone could not hold the Living Stone. We are called to train our hearts and minds to look for Jesus where He promises to be and to look for God in His primary work. Jesus is not spiteful and is not ready to punish with hardship. Jesus is not lying in wait, ready to make us stumble or to crush us. Jesus is the Living Stone that builds up those who trust in Him.[5]

Enemies of the Living Stone appear, by all outward appearances, to be winning. We long for Jesus to crush evil once and for all. He has and He does! Faith in the Living Stone is where we rest in all circumstances. We cling to His promise and we train our hearts and eyes and minds to cling to the truth. Jesus gently asks, "Have you never read the Scriptures?" The Scriptures foretold that Jesus would crush Satan. The Scriptures foretold that Jesus would face rejection and death. The Scriptures foretold that Jesus would not stay behind the stone of the tomb.

---

5 Religion breeds a culture of unhealthy guilt and shame. Those raised in a confusing culture where the law of God and the mercy of God have been mixed and misused must carefully discern the healthy and unhealthy aspects of what they have been taught about Christ's Word and work. The Living Stone offers life and offers rich opportunity to shed the unhealthy and embrace the life of Christ.

Jesus fulfilled the promises of the Scriptures then, and He continues to fulfill those promises. Faith embraces living in Christ, alive, growing, and continually being built up with all of the other stones whose faith is in Christ. Faith says that this world is not home. Our home is **in** Christ, the true Vine, the Living Stone. The stones that reject Christ will be crushed in God's time and in God's way. "Vengeance is Mine," says the Lord (Romans 12:19). We are free to live more fully, to delight in Christ's work of perfect righteousness, and to embrace Christ's work of perfect justice when we trust God's Word and work in this world and in us.

The Scriptures reveal Christ as the cornerstone and the keystone, the first and last stones of the building that is continually being built up with living stones. He is our foundation and the foundation of the whole body of believers; He is the finishing stone of our lives and of the building He is building. He, as crushing stone, has defeated and has the final say over evil, sin, and death in this world. We are engaged in a continual building project with all other living stones through Christ, the cornerstone and keystone.

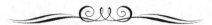

For individual study, meditate on the following questions and additional Scriptures. For small-group study, discuss these questions:

1. What has Christ as cornerstone and keystone revealed to you through these pages? What additional thoughts or Scripture verses came to your mind and heart as you meditated on these words?

2. How does Christ revealed as cornerstone help you grow in faith? How does Christ revealed as keystone help you grow in faith?

3. For further study, review Jesus' parables in Matthew 21, the two sons and the parable of the vineyard tenants. Religious leaders were the subjects of these parables, but they apply to all followers of the Christ. How does this help us understand our place as living stones?

4. Wrestle with the concepts of the alien (unknown, strange, peculiar, foreign) work of God contrasted with the proper work of God. Challenge yourself to see "God for us" in His life-giving, life-building work, and be built up as living stones in the spiritual house of God.

Chapter Six

Rock

Every rock is unique in both shape and size. Every rock is a solid mineral, a geologic formation. Some are crystalline forms, with many flat, repeating surfaces, while others are less orderly. Unique chemical makeup, crystals, minerals, elements, and atoms are just a few complex topics that are familiar to rock lovers and rock experts. The uniqueness of one rock as compared with another, the complexity of rock, is as astounding as the sheer volume of rocks.

Rocks—on the surface of the earth, below the surface, and deep in the molten core—form the foundation of this earth. Tiny rocks make up the soil of farmable rock. The floor of the oceans and seas and riverbed is made of rock, which holds the waters in place. Much of the earth's surface is sheer rock, unlivable.

Rocks are foundational in my life. I've played with them, tripped over them, scaled them, skipped them on ponds and rivers, built fortresses with them, carved them, and collected them. Rocks adorn my home and my yard as intentional reminders of God, the Rock of my salvation. I've

The view of Morro Rock (Morro Bay, California), from the vantage point of a canoe.

placed, as best I can, my burdens in them and laid them in row 124 in my vineyard as a visual reminder that God invites me to cast my cares on Him.

The Great Wall of China is a magnificent use of rock! Construction began in the third century BC and continued for centuries. The Great Wall is said to be 5,500 miles long, although much of it has deteriorated. For context, it is 2,800 miles from Los Angeles to New York, so the length of the Great Wall of China is equal to traveling across the width of the United States and back! In places, the base of the wall is fifteen to twenty feet wide, and the wall itself is fifteen to thirty feet tall, with thousands of watchtowers towering above the wall.

Lalibela, Ethiopia, is home to eleven distinctive rock churches. They were carved out of a mountain, a monolithic rock. Excavation (these churches were not constructed) began in the twelfth century AD. Each is unique, displaying the Christian faith through crosses and artistry depicting an understanding of the Gospel. They're a breathtaking sight! These small rock churches, while a great tourist attraction, have been home to worship services since their completion centuries ago.

One of eleven rock churches hewn from a monolithic rock in Lalibela, Ethiopia.

Rocks on mountains were hiding places for those fleeing from enemies. Rocks were used to build fortresses and places of refuge. They were used to build monuments, places of remembrance of the work of God in the midst of the people. Rocks were used as geographic markers, and they were carved and hewn and chiseled for specific purposes. Rocks were employed as shields and weapons.

Our modern world, with every convenience, is removed from rocks as people knew them when the Scriptures were written. Are we so removed from rock that these Scriptures don't have an impact on us or meaning for us? We're not so far removed as it might seem. Rock is all around us; it is simply repurposed as brick or cement or asphalt or steel. Rock in its raw form may not surround us, but it is under us, and we are most certainly surrounded by manufactured rock. We focus our attention on the use of the word *rock* and the images of rock in the Scriptures in order to grow in our understanding of and faith in the triune God.

The Diving Board
on top of Half Dome
(Yosemite), nearly five
thousand feet above
the valley floor, offers
hikers a thrilling view.

God is indescribable and incomprehensible, yet He wants us to know Him in a personal way so that our hearts and lives are drawn to Him. We use theological words such as omnipotent, omnipresent, and omniscient to describe God as all-powerful, ever-present, and all-knowing. Using weighty words has a place. Using imagery that surrounds us day by day is how authors of the Scriptures also revealed God for the people. Rocks surrounded them, so the imagery was easy to understand.

We are surrounded by rock too, in many forms, so we will take a look at Old Testament verses where God is likened to rock in order to draw us into deeper understanding. We will briefly explore the words of three individuals—Hannah, Moses, and David—with the understanding that there are many more rich stories in the Scriptures from which we could draw similar themes.

No Rock Like Our God: Hannah's Story

Hannah was a faithful woman of God. Her enemies had mocked her for being unable to bear children; she was devastated, and at one point, she was so sad and depressed that she wasn't taking care of herself. She cried out to God from her soul day and night (1 Samuel 1). Then, after many years of being barren, she gave birth to Samuel. She believed Samuel was a precious gift from God, so she dedicated his life to the service of the Lord.

When her baby was weaned, she took him to Eli in the temple. This is a portion of her song: "My heart exults in the Lord; my horn is exalted in the Lord. My mouth derides my enemies, because I rejoice in Your salvation. There is none holy like the Lord: for there is none besides You; there is no rock like our God" (1 Samuel 2:1–2). Her "salvation" was bearing a child that she immediately gave back to God.

Surrounded by the towering rocks in Israel, the monuments of old that marked the places of God's deliverance, Hannah declared, "There is no rock like our God." When I pick up a unique rock, I ponder her words, "There is no rock like our God." When I climbed Half Dome, I reflected, "There is no rock like our God." When I stepped out onto the Top of the Rock deck high above New York City—Rockefeller Center in Manhattan—I gasped and said, "There is no rock like our God."

Hannah's story and subsequent prayer using the image of the rock draws us closer to God, which is His holy desire for us. What causes us to cry out with our soul to God? What keeps us from crying out with our soul to God? Pick up rocks. Reflect on their unique shapes and sizes, their color and facets, their weight. Reflect on Hannah's words, "There is no rock like our God!" Speak Hannah's words of faith.

NO ROCK LIKE OUR GOD: MOSES' STORY

Moses led the children of Israel out of slavery in Egypt and through the desert wanderings for forty years. God worked His faithfulness through Moses time and time again. The children of Israel were weary and thirsty; they grumbled at God and at Moses. "Therefore the people quarreled with Moses and said, 'Give us water to drink.' And Moses said to them, 'Why do you quarrel with me? Why do you test the LORD?' But the people thirsted there for water, and the people grumbled against Moses and said, 'Why did you bring us up out of Egypt, to kill us and our children and our livestock with thirst?'" (Exodus 17:2–3). God responded to the cry of the people:

> And the LORD said to Moses, "Pass on before the people, taking with you some of the elders of Israel, and take in your hand the staff with which you struck the Nile, and go. Behold, I will stand before you there on the rock at Horeb, and you shall strike the rock, and water shall come out of it, and the people will drink." And Moses did so, in the sight of the elders of Israel. And he called the name of the

place Massah and Meribah, because of the quarreling of the people of Israel, and because they tested the LORD by saying, "Is the LORD among us or not?" Exodus 17:5–7

Moses named the place to remind the people of God's faithfulness in the form of a question: "Is the Lord among us or not?" The name continually reminded the people that God's faithfulness was bigger, greater than their grumbling. Years later, the thirsty people grumbled against Moses and God again:

> Would that we had perished when our brothers perished before the LORD! Why have you brought the assembly of the LORD into this wilderness, that we should die here, both we and our cattle? And why have you made us come up out of Egypt to bring us to this evil place? It is no place for grain or figs or vines or pomegranates, and there is no water to drink. Numbers 20:3–5

God heard their cries and gave Moses specific instructions to speak to the rock, to tell it to yield water. Rather than follow God's command, Moses struck the rock with his staff, as he had done in the previous instance. God brought water forth from the rock for the thirsty people despite Moses' disobedience. Here is the story:

> "Take the staff, and assemble the congregation, you and Aaron your brother, and tell the rock before their eyes to yield its water. So you shall bring water out of the rock for them and give drink to the congregation and their cattle." And Moses took the staff from before the LORD, as He commanded him. Then Moses and Aaron gathered the assembly together before the rock, and he said to them, "Hear now, you rebels: shall we bring water for you out of this rock?" And Moses lifted up his hand and struck

the rock with his staff twice, and water came out abundantly, and the congregation drank, and their livestock. Numbers 20:8–11

God faithfully brought forth water from the rock to quench the thirst of the people. His justice, however, demanded punishment for Moses and Aaron's disobedience. God spoke these words:

> "Because you did not believe in Me, to uphold Me as holy in the eyes of the people of Israel, therefore you shall not bring this assembly into the land that I have given them." These are the waters of Meribah, where the people of Israel quarreled with the LORD, and through them He showed Himself holy. Numbers 20:12–13

God named this place Meribah in order to remind the stubborn people that the Lord is holy. Despite the grumbling of the people and Moses' disobedience, God showed Himself holy and granted salvation through the rock and the water. Moses received punishment: he would die before passing over into the Promised Land. Moses accepted that and spoke these words as he passed leadership over to Joshua in the presence of the people:

> For I will proclaim the name of the LORD; ascribe greatness to our God! "The Rock, His work is perfect, for all His ways are justice. A God of faithfulness and without iniquity, just and upright is He." . . . For their rock is not as our Rock; our enemies are by themselves. Deuteronomy 32:3–4, 31

At the end of his life, Moses declared God's faithfulness, justice, and perfection. He trusted that God's faithfulness abounded even as he faced his final moments on the earth, short of his goal. He would not lead the people into the Promised Land. Nevertheless, Moses lives forever in the presence of God in the promised land of heaven, because God is faithful to His Word.

As we face challenging circumstances, illness, and death, and as those around us face the same, we are called to proclaim with Moses, "God is a God of faithfulness, perfect and just." We are called to learn that God punished Adam and Eve with death for their original sin and we have inherited that punishment. We are also called to learn that God's perfect justice was satisfied when His only Son breathed His final breath. Yes, we will die, but in Christ, we live today and for eternity. Rocks remind us to fix our eyes on Jesus, the Rock, who satisfies our thirst, sustains our lives, and is our righteousness and perfection.

No Rock Like Our God: David's Story

David was a warrior, a leader, and king over Israel. David recorded his stories and his struggles, his prayers and praises, in both beautiful and challenging psalms. He poured his heart out in times of both great distress and great rejoicing. Many of David's reflections use imagery of God as rock because rocks were his shield and hiding place when he fled from his enemies. David saw the unique beauty of rocks as well as their strength.

The following Scripture verses reveal David's faith in God, his Rock. I have chosen only a few for our reflection. Read these, take them to heart as your own, pray them, and memorize them.

- David spoke to the Lord the words of this song on the day when the LORD delivered him from the hand of all his enemies, and from the hand of Saul. He said, "The LORD is my rock and my fortress and my deliverer, my God, my rock, in whom I take refuge, my shield, and the horn of my salvation, my stronghold and my refuge, my savior; You save me from violence. I call upon the LORD, who is worthy to be praised, and I am saved from my enemies." 2 Samuel 22:1–4

- This God—His way is perfect; the word of the LORD proves true; He is a shield for all those who take refuge in Him. "For who is God, but the LORD? And who is a rock, except our God? This God is my strong refuge and has made my way blameless. . . . The LORD lives, and blessed be my rock, and exalted be my God, the rock of my salvation." 2 Samuel 22:31–33, 47

- I love You, O LORD, my strength. The LORD is my rock and my fortress and my deliverer, my God, my rock, in whom I take refuge, my shield, and the horn of my salvation, my stronghold. I call upon the LORD, who is worthy to be praised, and I am saved from my enemies. . . . For who is God, but the LORD? And who is a rock, except our God?—the God who equipped me with strength and made my way blameless. Psalm 18:1–3, 31–32

- In You, O LORD, do I take refuge; let me never be put to shame; in Your righteousness deliver me! Incline Your ear to me; rescue me speedily! Be a rock of refuge for me, a strong fortress to save me! For You are my rock and my fortress; and for Your name's sake You lead me and guide me. Psalm 31:1–3

- For God alone my soul waits in silence; from Him comes my salvation. He alone is my rock and my salvation, my fortress; I shall not be greatly shaken. . . . He only is my rock and my salvation, my fortress; I shall not be shaken. On God rests my salvation and my glory; my mighty rock, my refuge is God. Trust in Him at all times, O people; pour out your heart before Him; God is a refuge for us. Psalm 62:1–2, 6–8

Salvation is a key theme throughout these and many other "Rock" verses. In order to grasp David's heart, God's heart, through these verses, we may need to broaden our definition of salvation. Salvation means eternal life when we die and so much more! Salvation is eternity in Christ now. Salvation is aliveness; it is freedom to be alive, to live. Salvation means delivery, liberty, help, freedom, victory. Salvation is God's mercy and love in action. David was delivered, rescued, and saved from the enemy in his rock fortress to live life. We are delivered, rescued, and saved from the enemy to live life. The rocks were David's salvation; the Rock, Christ, was David's salvation; the Rock, Christ, is our salvation.

David's writing was so profound because he articulated many life experiences in which he could trust in God ONLY for salvation. David had nowhere else to turn; he was at the end; he had no hope except in God's deliverance. David's story is unique, so filled with warfare and swords and enemies that his words may not resonate with us. Yet our lives are filled with joys and challenges, pain and suffering, warfare and enemies too! Just like David, we are called to visualize and cry out to the Rock as salvation and deliverer.

There will come a day when we must trust God fully with our lives. When we are on our deathbed and breathing our last, we will be called to full trust in God alone, our Rock, our Deliverer. All of our earthly life and daily living is practice for that last earthly day. Will we be able to see with eyes of faith that in spite of all outward appearances of defeat, we—by passing into death—are passing through death into eternal life? Eternal life is ours, a reality of every day in Christ throughout our earthly life.

God's call to us through David's words is that we cling to the truth of these words today. We are living the story of God's salvation history. Death has been defeated; evil has lost. Still, we must ask ourselves, are we truly living? Are we alive or are we wandering like the children of Israel, who were very religious and had been delivered from physical slavery but were not free because their hearts were hard to the work of salvation? They had been freed and we have been freed to live in freedom, victory, and liberty under the cross of Christ, who suffered, died, and lived that we truly live.

Cindy and Cecy pause
as they approach
Half Dome for the
ascent, September 2011.

CHRIST, THE ROCK THAT FOLLOWED: THE APOSTLE PAUL'S WORDS

The apostle Paul referenced rock only twice in his letters. The first reference expounded on Christ as a rock of offense. Paul quoted Psalm 118, Isaiah 8, and Isaiah 28, and unfolded the rich meaning of the Old Testament:

> What shall we say, then? That Gentiles who did not pursue righteousness have attained it, that is, a righteousness that is by faith; but that Israel who pursued a law that would lead to righteousness did not succeed in reaching that law. Why? Because they did not pursue it by faith, but as if it were based on works. They have stumbled over the stumbling stone, as it is written, "Behold, I am laying in Zion a stone of stumbling, and a rock of offense; and whoever believes in Him will not be put to shame." Romans 9:30–33

Paul argued that faith in Christ based on the Law is not faith at all. Faith in the man Jesus Christ is founded on the fulfillment of promises foretold in the Old Testament. He is a rock of offense to those who would not receive God's work through His life and work. Christ is a stumbling stone to those who pursue righteousness apart from His holy life and righteousness.

The second reference to rock is in Paul's letter to the people of Corinth. He called them to do everything to the glory of God, to cherish life, to not be enslaved by the things of this world but to live life in Christ as saved people. Paul called the people of God to a life of discipline as a sign of faith in Christ. Paul's call was not to enslave a free people or free an enslaved people. Freedom to live life freely was an expression of gratitude, an act of worship. Paul drew the Old Testament story of the rock providing water for thirsty people, with a bright new insight, into his discussion of freedom in Christ:

> For I do not want you to be unaware, brothers, that our fathers were all under the cloud, and all passed through the sea, and all were baptized into Moses in the cloud and in the sea, and all ate the same spiritual food, and all drank the same spiritual drink. For they drank from the spiritual Rock that followed them, and the Rock was Christ.
> 1 Corinthians 10:1–4

The drink that cannot satisfy is sharply contrasted with the drink from the Rock that satisfies in Paul's letter to the people of Corinth. The drink that cannot satisfy, Paul declared, is idol worship, serving the desires of the flesh, living outside one's calling, abusing the gifts of God, lording power over others, and so forth. The drink that satisfies is Christ, the Rock, who was with the people in the desert, providing living water, and was with the woman at the well, providing living water. Christ the spiritual rock is with us, providing living water.

Within the Church, people were seeking to live both in freedom in Christ and in the immorality of the world. Paul made the message clear: Salvation, in the fullest sense of the word, leads to lives of gratitude and unselfish living. Salvation leads to growth in faith and love toward God God, neighbor, and self. Salvation trusts that the Lord is present among us and deeply desires that we live life in Christ, grafted into His holy life in us. Christ cries out, "Live life, perfectly bound and perfectly free in Me, as an expression of worship without fear or shame."

Contrast the Messiah in the mind of the religious leaders with the Christ, born of the Virgin Mary, the Christ who healed the sick and raised the dead, the Christ who suffered, died, and rose from the grave. The religious leaders had plenty of idols, including the temple, knowledge, traditions, laws, and rules. Christ freely gave mercy, love, forgiveness, and healing to those who looked to Him as the rock and deliverer, the living water that satisfies thirst.

CHRIST, THE ROCK THAT FOLLOWED

The spiritual Rock that followed the people in the desert was the Son of God, the Rock from whom living water flowed. Paul connected Christ to the rock that satisfied the thirst of the wandering people of Israel. The apostle John recorded Jesus' words and actions in the story of the woman at the well. The Samaritan woman experienced and received Christ as salvation, deliverer. We know the story, but ponder it in light of the spiritual Rock, who provides living water:

> A woman from Samaria came to draw water. Jesus said to her, "Give Me a drink." (For His disciples had gone away into the city to buy food.) The Samaritan woman said to Him, "How is it that You, a Jew, ask for a drink from me, a woman of Samaria?" (For Jews have no dealings with Samaritans.) Jesus answered her, "If you knew the gift of God, and who it is that is saying to you, 'Give Me a drink,' you would have asked Him, and He would have given you living water." John 4:7–10

Quite certainly the woman did not comprehend Jesus' words at the beginning of their conversation. Her eyes were opened when Jesus got to the broken places in her heart and spoke life and salvation into those places. Life flowed from Jesus' words, so much so that the woman returned to her town and testified to salvation in Christ. Christ's words freed her and many in her community to live fully, freely, in deliverance and in true worship:

> [She said,] "Our fathers worshiped on this mountain, but you say that in Jerusalem is the place where people ought to worship." Jesus said to her, "Woman, believe Me, the hour is coming when neither on this mountain nor in Jerusalem will you worship the Father. You worship what

you do not know; we worship what we know, for salvation is from the Jews. But the hour is coming, and is now here, when the true worshipers will worship the Father in spirit and truth, for the Father is seeking such people to worship Him. God is spirit, and those who worship Him must worship in spirit and truth." The woman said to Him, "I know that Messiah is coming (He who is called Christ). When He comes, He will tell us all things." Jesus said to her, "I who speak to you am He." John 4:20–26

Jesus not only bridged the old, as revealed in these verses, but He also fulfilled the Old Testament promises, commands and demands. Jesus' powerful words, "I who speak to you am He," call our hearts into a journey of faith that goes deeper than what we've known and that takes us into worship in spirit and truth by simply receiving Christ at His word. Our worship is not defined by a building made of rock or the traditions within that building, but rather by the Rock, who calls us to Himself. Christ's mercy shapes our building; Christ's mercy shapes our traditions and our worship. We receive through the hearing of the Word; we are freed; we grow; we share with one another and this world.

The progression in this chapter of John's Gospel directly connected God's desire for all people to hear His Word and the Old Testament to the present moment with the woman at the well. Jesus and His disciples were passing through Samaria instead of traveling around the "unclean" area, as was customary. Jesus spoke to a Samaritan woman—something unheard of, even forbidden in His day. Jesus was at a well that had been dug by Jacob, the father of Israel. Jesus asked the woman for a drink of water. Jesus proclaimed Himself living water, and offered Himself to her as deliverance. Jesus discussed true worship, worship in spirit and truth, with the Samaritan woman while the disciples were away buying food.

The Samaritan woman is often spoken of as an outcast of society, but we don't know her story. If she were truly an outcast, why did the people of her community listen to her and come to faith through her testimony? Why did they follow her out to the well to meet Jesus? She was educated, as she knew that the fathers of Israel worshiped there on that mountain and that the Jews said that true worship took place in Jerusalem. The woman carried on an extended conversation with Jesus, during which she revealed knowledge and faith that the Christ was coming. She boldly stated to Christ, "He will tell *us* all things." She received Jesus at His word and then proclaimed what she heard in her community.

PETER'S BOLD CONFESSION: THE ROCK UPON WHICH CHRIST BUILDS HIS CHURCH

Peter and the disciples were asked by Jesus, "Who do you say I am?" Peter's bold reply to Jesus' question and His answer to Peter give us much to uncover as we conclude this chapter of *The Rock Speaks*. Jesus' question "Who do you say I am?" is vitally important for us to answer. We need a clear answer to Jesus' question. Our culture and our modern world beg an authentic answer of us; the Church needs a clear answer to Jesus' question. Here is Matthew's record of the conversation:

> Now when Jesus came into the district of Caesarea Philippi, He asked His disciples, "Who do people say that the Son of Man is?" And they said, "Some say John the Baptist, others say Elijah, and others Jeremiah or one of the prophets." He said to them, "But who do you say that I am?" Simon Peter replied, "You are the Christ, the Son of the living God." And Jesus answered him, "Blessed are you, Simon Bar-Jonah! For flesh and blood has not revealed this to you, but My Father who is in heaven. And I tell you, you

are Peter, and on this rock I will build My church, and the
gates of hell shall not prevail against it." Matthew 16:13–18

Christ, the Rock, stated that He would build His Church on Peter's
reply, "You are the Christ, the Son of the living God." Simon saw Jesus,
believed Him, and confessed Him as the Christ. Jesus gave Simon a new
name, Peter, and called him blessed because of his bold confession. Peter's
heart is revealed in his letters that call us to trust that Christ is the cornerstone and we are living stones being built up in Him, a spiritual house.

Christ is the Rock. Peter's true confession is the rock upon which
Christ would build His Church. Christ said, "You are Peter, and on this
rock I will build My church." Christ built and is building the Church on
Peter's confession of the Christ. The Church is the Body of Christ, and we
are being built up in Christ on Peter's confession of the Christ. Christ calls
the Church to be His Body, to confess, "You are the Christ."

What do we think of when we are asked, "What is the Church?" We
might think of *church* as a building or a denomination. While that is
entirely true, there is so much more! We don't worship Peter—we worship the Christ whom Peter confessed. We don't worship our building, but
rather, our building serves as a gathering place to worship the Christ and
receive His gifts through Word and Sacrament.

The Church is built on Peter's bold confession of Jesus, not on Peter
the man. The story that follows in Matthew's Gospel confirms that the
Church can only ever be built on Christ (not on man) and on the confession of the Christ. Matthew records:

> From that time Jesus began to show His disciples that He
> must go to Jerusalem and suffer many things from the el-
> ders and chief priests and scribes, and be killed, and on the
> third day be raised. And Peter took Him aside and began
> to rebuke Him, saying, "Far be it from You, Lord! This shall

never happen to You." But He turned and said to Peter, "Get behind Me, Satan! You are a hindrance to Me. For you are not setting your mind on the things of God, but on the things of man." Matthew 16:21–23

Peter wanted to protect Jesus from harm, from suffering and death. Jesus didn't welcome Peter's noble attempt at kindness or protection or control. When Peter tried to control His word and work, even though he was trying to protect Him, Jesus rebuked him harshly. In the span of just a few short verses in Matthew's Gospel, Peter is called "blessed" for his confession of the Christ and rebuked for trying to control Jesus' path to the cross.

Rocks remind us that the Rock is the only rock upon which the Church is built. Christ is cornerstone and keystone, the alpha and omega. The Rock calls us to live our faith in Him at every moment. Just as we live in our body every moment, we live in His Body every moment, not just on Sunday mornings when we go to church. The Rock calls us to boldly answer His question, "Who do you say I am?" Like Peter, we declare, "You are the Christ, the Rock, the Son of the living God." What are we really saying? What might this mean for you and me today as we journey deeper into faith in Christ?

- Open the Scriptures and "see" with our eyes and hearts the rock of the Old Testament, Christ the Rock in the New Testament, for us and in us.

- Pray that God would open our hearts and minds to receive Him at His Word, to live in faith grafted into His holy life through Baptism and to receive His body and blood to nourish and cleanse us.

- Dig deep into the Word and allow His work to soften our hearts, calm our fears, and give us courage to cling to Him for life.

- Place ourselves into the stories of Jesus' walk on this earth. Receive Jesus like the woman at the well, the blind, the lame, the deaf, Peter, John, the dead.

- Answer Jesus' question, "What do you want me to do for you?" Ask, receive, give!

Rocks, whether in natural form or in the form of modern buildings or roads or other structures, remind us to dig more deeply into the image of God as rock. Pray with Hannah, "There is no rock like our God!" With Moses we declare that God, our Rock, is faithful, just, and upright. Expand on David's list of God as Rock, Refuge, Fortress, Deliverer, Salvation. With Peter we declare, "You are the Christ." We are built up on the Rock, God our Father and Christ, His Son, through the Holy Spirit of the living God.

For individual study, meditate on the following questions. For small-group study, discuss these questions:

1. What has God as the Rock and Christ as the Rock revealed to you through these pages? What additional thoughts or Scripture verses came to your mind and heart as you meditated on these words?

2. How does Christ revealed as the Rock that followed the Israelites in the desert help you grow in faith? How do these words challenge you to grow?

3. How can we as members of the Church, the Body of Christ here on earth and for all eternity, witness Christ, the Rock, to the world?

South Fork Cave Creek in
the Chiricahua Mountains
of Arizona.

Chapter Seven

HILLS AND CAVES

The rolling hills of the Central Coast of California are my home. My great-grandparents chose to build the house in which I now live a hundred feet from a creek bank that drops fifteen feet, the lowest spot on the property. The soil is fertile. The drainage runs from the hills around my house to the creek. The rolling hills, which were planted with grain or dotted with cattle in the past, are now covered with grapevines. When I was a child, the hills were my playground. As children, my brother and I loved riding in the Jeep with Dad as he bounced over the hills. That same Jeep is the vehicle we use today for guided tours of Steinbeck Vineyards.

Jeep tours of the property begin at our tasting room and meander up and down the gentle rolling hills through the vineyards on our six-hundred-acre property. Midway through the tour, we climb the steepest hill, which we lovingly call "Grandma's Hill." The view is breathtaking! Up to this point in the tour, our guests' focus has been on individual vines, the hills, and the steep climb. Then, at the top of Grandma's Hill, our eyes and senses are filled with the 360-degree view of our community. To the north, we can see beyond the Monterey County line; south and west are

The rolling hills of central California near Paso Robles.

the Santa Lucia Mountains, which separate us from California's coastline; and to the east we look toward California's Central Valley.

Conversations about vineyard practices, family stories, and how the weather affects us each year abound as we bounce over miles of vineyard roads in our 1958 Willys Jeep. Pausing to visit amid the vines is common. First-time visitors hold on tight as we rev up the Jeep to climb Grandma's Hill. Not knowing what to expect, they gasp at the view from the top. Often we are asked, "Do you ever get tired of this?" "Never!" is our reply. Returning guests bring friends, so the conversation is different. When we approach the hill, they declare, "This is what I was telling you about!" They bring their friends to experience the vineyard AND the Jeep ride up and down Grandma's Hill AND the view from the top.

The perspective of the vineyard varies drastically from the low spots looking out and up to the top of the hill looking down and out. One view is close up; the other is 360

degrees. After rain, we cannot take the Jeep up Grandma's Hill because of the slippery clay mud. We know there is so much more, but first-time guests experience so much and they don't know about the "more" they are missing. We may tell them about the view and point to where we will take them on their next trip, but it isn't the same as experiencing the climb and the view.

The soil on our hills is sandy loam, which would be plantable soil if the hills were not so steep. We don't have caves here (although I'm told that years ago, there was a cave on the property that has since collapsed). Many hills around the world are laced with caves, which form in rock composite of limestone, dolomite, and gypsum. Minerals in the dripping water form stalactites down from the roofs of caves and stalagmites up from the floors of caves.

I have childhood memories of caving with my dad in the Carlsbad Caverns. The dark and damp descent down the steep, slippery stairs and ladders took forever in my young mind. The smell and the feeling of climbing deep into the earth were scary and exhilarating. The cave was huge! Bright lights on the floor lit the cave, and we could see the incredible stalactite and stalagmite formations. I remember the sound of water dripping and the feeling of breathing in the damp, heavy air.

I've also caved on White Chief Mountain in the Sequoias, where headlamps and much caution are needed in the unexplored caves. Climbing up out of caves into the bright, blinding sunlight and my first breath of fresh air is as distinct a memory as the look of relief on my mom's anxious face. Mom hadn't gone down into the cave with us. She knew it was dangerous, and her fear that we might not come out was real. Her relief was real too.

Exploration of hills and caves is the basis for this chapter as we explore God's call to deeper faith and trust in His word and work for us, in us, and through us. Hills were important for survival; hills were a place of teaching for Jesus; and hills provided rich imagery as people were called to deeper faith by the authors of the Scriptures. Caves were also necessary for survival when they were used as hiding places. And caves were used as tombs. As with sand and soil, stone and rock, the authors of the Scriptures told stories and drew pictures with language to help us see God's mercy, love, protection, and deliverance more clearly.

To the Hills

My favorite place on our property is the top of Grandma's Hill. Hiking from my house to the hill is my preferred method of transportation. As I'm walking, I pay attention to the path in front of me, to each step on the rocky roads. I also pay attention to my goal: the top of the hill. I focus on both the view immediately in front and the view farther away at the hilltop. When I'm feeling a lot of stress or sadness, I look down, shoulders heavy with the weight of my emotions. Realizing that, I consciously take deep breaths, roll my shoulders back, and raise my eyes to the hill. Learning to recognize the weight and then change my posture has been a challenging process of growth.

As I walk and think, my heart is drawn to some of my favorite words from the Psalms: "I lift up my eyes to the hills. From where does my help come? My help comes from the LORD, who made heaven and earth" (Psalm 121:1–2). Deep guidance flows from these verses. The author has learned to lift his eyes in times when help is needed. He doesn't say, "I've got it all together, so I know to lift my eyes to the hills." He says, "Here is what I know and do when I need help." The remainder of this short chapter shifts from the author stating what he knows to work in tough times, to words of wisdom "for you":

> I lift up my eyes to the hills. From where does my help come? My help comes from the LORD, who made heaven and earth. He will not let your foot be moved; He who keeps you will not slumber. Behold, He who keeps Israel will neither slumber nor sleep. The LORD is your keeper; the LORD is your shade on your right hand. The sun shall not strike you by day, nor the moon by night. The LORD will keep you from all evil; He will keep your life. The LORD will keep your going out and your coming in from this time forth and forevermore. Psalm 121

During times of pain and sadness, we tend to see faith in God's work in a narrow sense. We look at what's immediately before us. This little picture can be less hopeful, more painful, and can sometimes seem as though it will not pass. God says, "Lift your eyes to the hills; lift your eyes to Me, and fix them on Me. Trust that My word and work are for you and in you." Lifting our eyes brings a different perspective, a panoramic view.

Ponder a little child who has done wrong. With proper guidance, the child says, "I'm sorry," and is forgiven by parents. The child's eyes look down, his heart still sad, when a kind daddy places his giant hand under the child's chin and gently lifts the head up. The child's gaze meets the parent's eyes, and they communicate, "I love you." Picture yourself and understand that this is true for all of us, that in times of deep distress or sorrow or anger, it is challenging for us to lift our eyes to the hills to look for mercy and help outside ourselves. Yet faith looks up and out; faith declares, "Our help comes from the LORD!"

The great warrior David wrote these powerful words after he escaped from his son Absalom and thousands of others who were trying to take his life. In distress he cried out, cried aloud to the Lord:

> O LORD, how many are my foes! Many are rising against me; many are saying of my soul, there is no salvation for him in God. But You, O LORD, are a shield about me, my glory, and the lifter of my head. I cried aloud to the LORD, and He answered me from His holy hill. Psalm 3:1–4

While we may not have thousands of enemies chasing us from all sides, we have much in common with David. Do we have foes? Are many saying, "Salvation can't be for you"? Maybe not to this extreme, but then again, what is our inner talk? What is our mind saying? What are our thoughts when we lie down to rest? Are we our own enemy because of lies we've believed about ourselves? Are we our own enemy because of untruth or partial truth we believe about God? For example, do we believe that God helps those who help themselves? Do we believe that God will help others and has saved others but question if He would do so for us? Do we believe that emotions are wrong? Do we believe anger is wrong? Do we believe we are wrong, just for being?

Extreme? I don't think so!

Is it hard to be honest and admit that we have minds that speak this way in the quiet moments? Yes.

Maybe family members who should have taught us to lift our head by gently guiding us were those who hurt us most deeply. Maybe we have a really tough time believing that God our heavenly Father is *for* us. Maybe the Church has hurt us deeply. The list goes on and on. Thank God that His mercy is bigger than our fear and our pain. We believe and trust that Jesus has more for us. Thank God that He invites us to cry out, to trust. God calls us to lift our eyes to Him!

When we are challenged to lift our eyes to the hills, we meditate on David's profound words, "But You, O LORD, are a shield about me, my glory, and the lifter of my head." David's anguish was real and it was deep. He knew God was his protection, his salvation, and the lifter of his head. David needed God to lift his head so that he was able to see God's answer of mercy and salvation from His holy hill.

We need the Maker of the heavens and the earth to lift our heads. We need to learn to cry out to God and trust that He is for *us*, working at all times, despite the circumstances that cause our heads and eyes to be down. The journey of life provides continual opportunities to practice trusting and to grow. The hills teach us that we need a broad view, the big picture. God lifts our head and our eyes to the hills.

We want and need to see Jesus when our heads, eyes, and hearts are down. We also need one another for courage, encouragement, and strength. We need trusted friends to walk with us. There are times we need to reach out to those God puts in our life to work through, to help lift our head and view our life from a different perspective. Pastors, counselors, and therapists are people God works through.

FROM THE HILLS

Perspective from the hills changes everything. I've been to the top of Grandma's Hill hundreds of times and I never tire of the view. Feelings of joy and calm are my companions as I walk through the rolling hills. On those days, my walks are brisk and fun. There are also days of deep anguish and pain, a fear of the journey. On those days, my steps are heavier until I get to the top of Grandma's Hill. When I'm on top of the hill, looking out and down, I have a completely different perspective than when I'm in the middle of the vineyard or at the bottom of the hill.

Perspective from the hills changes everything! The Scriptures call us to see from the hills. The Psalms, for instance, are filled with words of hope and encouragement from the hills. God's Word calls us to embrace these words for us, to grow in faith and understanding, to live from a "head up, eyes up and out" perspective. Each of these references comes from the context of God's salvation, in the broadest sense as deliverance, liberty, help, freedom, and victory. These words call us to a grander perspective from the hills.

- By awesome deeds You answer us with righteousness, O God of our salvation, the hope of all the ends of the earth and of the farthest seas; . . . The pastures of the wilderness overflow, the hills gird themselves with joy, the meadows clothe themselves with flocks, the valleys deck themselves with grain, they shout and sing together for joy. Psalm 65:5, 12–13

- Give the king Your justice, O God, and Your righteousness to the royal son! May he judge your people with righteousness, and your poor with justice! Let the mountains bear prosperity for the people, and the hills, in righteousness! May he defend the cause of the poor of the people, give deliverance to the children of the needy, and crush the oppressor! Psalm 72:1–4

- Let the sea roar, and all that fills it; the world and those who dwell in it! Let the rivers clap their hands; let the hills sing for joy together before the LORD, for He comes to judge the earth. He will judge the world with righteousness, and the peoples with equity. Psalm 98:7–9

The psalmists declare that the hills gird themselves with joy, the hills bear righteousness, and the hills sing for joy. The hills call us to look up and out to see that the hills burst forth because the salvation of God is true and real. The hills burst forth because the righteousness of God is perfect and holy. The hills call us to look up and out to see that salvation and righteousness are for us, today, right here and now.

Jesus sat on the hillsides to teach and to feed people both bread and His words of life. The hills burst forth with joy as Jesus, the righteousness of God, revealed Himself to the people and for the people. While we cannot sit and receive at Jesus' feet on a grassy hill in Jerusalem, we can sit at Jesus' feet and receive His Word, the Scriptures.

Join me in this grand adventure! Receive Jesus' words from the hills. Be refreshed, restored, and renewed. Through Christ's Body, the Church, we receive and fellowship with one another. We confess, repent, and are restored. We claim our Baptism, receive forgiveness, and feast on Christ's holy body and blood for forgiveness and nourishment and life. Having received, we live life, hills all around us reminding us to lift our eyes. The Psalms reveal the very work of God that took place through the life of His Son. Christ's work continues for us and in us.

Our adventure may not include a knight in shining armor riding from the hills to sweep us up and carry us into a fairy tale of perfection according to our own definition. Jesus is Savior and Deliverer. Jesus is our righteousness and our salvation. Through His holy life, suffering, death, and resurrection, we are free to live life in our stories. Jesus redeems us.

Jesus has redeemed our entire story, all of it, past tense. From the hills, He teaches us, and He calls us to Himself through these words:

> Blessed are the poor in spirit, for theirs is the kingdom of heaven. Blessed are those who mourn, for they shall be comforted. Blessed are the meek, for they shall inherit the earth. Blessed are those who hunger and thirst for righteousness, for they shall be satisfied. Blessed are the merciful, for they shall receive mercy. Blessed are the pure in heart, for they shall see God. Blessed are the peacemakers, for they shall be called sons of God. Blessed are those who are persecuted for righteousness' sake, for theirs is the kingdom of heaven. Matthew 5:3–10

> You are the light of the world. A city set on a hill cannot be hidden. Nor do people light a lamp and put it under a basket, but on a stand, and it gives light to all in the house. In the same way, let your light shine before others, so that they may see your good works and give glory to your Father who is in heaven. Matthew 5:14–16

We listen carefully to Jesus as He speaks to us through these words from the hill. He calls us into the big picture to see Him as the kingdom of heaven in our midst, giving us His words of life and healing and wholeness. We are who He says we are because He is God and He gives the "blessedness" to us for His name's sake. We can let our light shine because we reflect Him, the light of the world.

Jesus teaches us that we cannot do His job to redeem ourselves through religion or through repentance or through good works. He teaches us from the hill that He is our hope, our righteousness:

> Do not think that I have come to abolish the Law or the Prophets; I have not come to abolish them but to fulfill

them. For truly, I say to you, until heaven and earth pass away, not an iota, not a dot, will pass from the Law until all is accomplished. Therefore whoever relaxes one of the least of these commandments and teaches others to do the same will be called least in the kingdom of heaven, but whoever does them and teaches them will be called great in the kingdom of heaven. For I tell you, unless your righteousness exceeds that of the scribes and Pharisees, you will never enter the kingdom of heaven. Matthew 5:17–20

The hills sing forth because the Creator of the hills, Jesus, spoke righteousness to the people and for the people. Jesus lived righteousness and fulfilled the Law perfectly. The adventure takes on rich meaning because at every hill, every valley, every mountain, we are called to trust Him and follow Him. The adventure is challenging because trust doesn't come naturally. Trust, like faith, is a gift from a generous Giver that grows with life experience through both joy and pain.

The hills teach us to listen with our hearts, to consider Matthew's words: "And when Jesus finished these sayings, the crowds were astonished at His teaching, for He was teaching them as one who had authority, and not as their scribes" (Matthew 7:28–29). From the hills, Jesus, the Word of God in the flesh, spoke the Word of God. We are called to sit with the Word, to listen to Jesus up close, and see ourselves in the adventure of God's salvation history.

Jesus didn't stay on the hills teaching. Jesus moved, He lived, He led. Jesus healed, Jesus cleansed, and Jesus raised the dead to life. People followed. Many received Jesus the Messiah in faith; some followed to entrap, to destroy, to purge the world of this man. When Jesus turned His face toward Jerusalem, His closest followers tried to protect Him from another hill—Calvary, the holy hill. We beg Jesus to teach us and to draw us closer to Him through God's holy hill.

GOD'S HOLY HILL

God's holy hill is also called "Zion," "Jerusalem," and "the city of David" in the Scriptures. Jerusalem, or Zion, was the dwelling place of God, amid the people of God. They had received the promises of God and looked for the promises to be fulfilled in the Messiah. A transfer of the holy place happened when Jesus began His earthly ministry. He, the Son of God, was the dwelling place of God. The holiness of God dwelled in Him. Jesus' work on God's holy hill was foretold in the Old Testament and unfolded in Jesus' life as His perfect life was sacrificed for the sins of the world.

The Messiah's perfect life and work on earth was accomplished through the angry actions of those who thought they were protecting God's holy hill. The prophets were murdered in Jerusalem, and Jesus would be too by religious leaders who tasked themselves with protecting their perception of God. The psalmist declares:

> Why do the nations rage and the peoples plot in vain? The kings of the earth set themselves, and the rulers take counsel together, against the LORD and against His Anointed, saying, "Let us burst their bonds apart and cast away their cords from us." He who sits in the heavens laughs; the Lord holds them in derision. Then He will speak to them in His wrath, and terrify them in His fury, saying, "As for Me, I have set My King on Zion, My holy hill." I will tell of the decree: The LORD said to Me, "You are My Son; today I have begotten You. Ask of Me, and I will make the nations Your heritage, and the ends of the earth Your possession." Psalm 2:1–8

The words "You are My Son" were spoken of Christ on a hill known as the Mount of Transfiguration. The disciples were there when God's Word from the heavens placed all authority on Christ.

> Behold, there appeared to them Moses and Elijah, talking with Him. And Peter said to Jesus, "Lord, it is good that we are here. If You wish, I will make three tents here, one for You and one for Moses and one for Elijah." He was still speaking when, behold, a bright cloud overshadowed them, and a voice from the cloud said, "This is My beloved Son, with whom I am well pleased; listen to Him." When the disciples heard this, they fell on their faces and were terrified. But Jesus came and touched them, saying, "Rise, and have no fear." And when they lifted up their eyes, they saw no one but Jesus only. Matthew 17:3–8

Peter interpreted the transfiguration this way: "For when He received honor and glory from God the Father, and the voice was borne to Him by the Majestic Glory, 'This is My beloved Son, with whom I am well pleased,' we ourselves heard this very voice borne from heaven, for we were with Him on the holy mountain" (2 Peter 1:17–18). The mountain was holy because the voice of God is holy and because Jesus is holy.

We are holy because Jesus is holy. Jesus calls us to look out from the top of the hill. The broad view expands our vision, our perspective on life. Christ's call to live life fully in Him is grounded in His authority to speak mercy, love, forgiveness, hope, and healing into our lives. We receive the promises of God that were fulfilled in Christ. He declares us holy; therefore we *are* holy. We are holy not because we have ascended some hill of perfection or repentance or serving, but because Jesus is holy.

We are holy because, when faced with suffering and eternal death, Jesus chose suffering and death for us. We are holy because God's justice was carried out on that holy hill where His innocent Son was murdered to fulfill His gracious will, spoken to Adam and Eve in the promise of deliverance. The holy hill of Calvary in Jerusalem was God's righteousness and justice carried out in full.

The prophet Daniel foretold this event and gives us a powerful prayer to pray as we grow in our understanding of Christ's fulfillment of God's work on Jerusalem's holy hill.

> O LORD, according to all Your righteous acts, let Your anger and Your wrath turn away from Your city Jerusalem, Your holy hill, because for our sins, and for the iniquities of our fathers, Jerusalem and Your people have become a byword among all who are around us. Now therefore, O our God, listen to the prayer of Your servant and to his pleas for mercy, and for Your own sake, O Lord, make Your face to shine upon Your sanctuary, which is desolate. O my God, incline Your ear and hear. Open Your eyes and see our desolations, and the city that is called by Your name. For we do not present our pleas before You because of our righteousness, but because of Your great mercy. O Lord, hear; O Lord, forgive. O Lord, pay attention and act. Delay not, for Your own sake, O my God, because Your city and Your people are called by Your name. Daniel 9:16–19

God's justice was carried out many years after Daniel spoke this plea to God on behalf of the people. We plead with God for understanding and faith to grasp the magnitude of His mercy in the gift of the holy life of His Son who willingly journeyed to the holy hill. We are confident to beg this of God, not because of our righteousness but because of God's great mercy.

God hears our cries, and we continue to learn to trust Him with our deepest cries. The righteous demands of God were fulfilled in Christ on Jerusalem's holy hill. That was not ever and will never be our work. We continue to learn to trust God with that too. God's plan was fulfilled through the precious, perfect life of His Son poured out for us. Thank God that Christ passed through the holy hill and through the cave for our salvation!

Through the Cave

The lifeless body of Lazarus lay in a cave. His sisters told Jesus that they knew he would rise on the Last Day, a testament to their faith in God's salvation work. Jesus declared, "I am the resurrection and the life" (John 11:25). Lazarus's salvation through the cave happened this way:

> Then Jesus, deeply moved again, came to the tomb. It was a cave, and a stone lay against it. Jesus said, "Take away the stone." Martha, the sister of the dead man, said to Him, "Lord, by this time there will be an odor, for he has been dead four days." Jesus said to her, "Did I not tell you that if you believed you would see the glory of God?" So they took away the stone. And Jesus lifted up His eyes and said, "Father, I thank You that You have heard Me. I knew that You always hear Me, but I said this on account of the people standing around, that they may believe that You sent Me." When He had said these things, He cried out with a loud voice, "Lazarus, come out." The man who had died came out, his hands and feet bound with linen strips, and his face wrapped with a cloth. Jesus said to them, "Unbind him, and let him go." John 11:38–44

The resurrection of Lazarus came through the cave and through Jesus' words, "Come forth" (KJV and NASB). Lazarus's dead body was given life through the Word of God. The resurrection of Jesus came through the cave. Jesus' lifeless body lay in the cave for three days. Jesus had called

Lazarus forth from death; now He Himself was dead in a cave with a large stone covering the entrance. God raised Jesus to life as He had promised He would do.

Lazarus passed through the cave to live life by Christ's Word; Jesus passed through the cave and was raised to life by His Father. Through the cave and by that resurrection, we, too, are raised to live life! What cave of deadness holds us in darkness? Fear? Doubt? Depression? Desperation? Lies? False belief that we must do the work of our own salvation? Belief that our value is in what we do, not who we are in Christ? Rebellion? Secrets? Misuse of drugs, alcohol, or food to bury our pain? Isolation? Hurtful self-talk? Hurtful talk of others?

Jesus cries out in a loud voice, "Come forth!" He calls us forth, calls us to pass through death into life by His life-giving Word. He works courage in us, bringing us to the place in our lives where we cry out from the cave for help. We are not alone. Jesus is with us and in us and for us. He calls us to look to the hills and trust that His help is near. He calls us to look to Him through the holy hill of Calvary.

Jesus, too, lay dead in a cave. God worked through the cross, through Christ's dying and death and through the cave to bring the resurrection as the fulfillment of His promises. The word and work of Christ is the same today, in our midst. Resurrection from death is real, not just some-day, but today in Christ's call. Today we listen to Christ's Word, heed His call to come forth, and trust that He will give us strength and courage. One day we will pass through the cave—the grave—and God's promises will be fully fulfilled for us. We pass through the cave into life *now, today,* because salvation is in our midst.

The darkness of the cave weighs heavy on us, yet there is light in the darkness, hope through the cave. God works through His Word and Sacraments as well as through people who have journeyed out of the darkness of the cave and into light. Peter witnessed the raising of Lazarus; Peter witnessed Jesus' life, suffering, and death. Peter witnessed Jesus being placed into the cave, and he saw the empty cave. Peter declared the living hope he witnessed, for us:

> Blessed be the God and Father of our Lord Jesus Christ! According to His great mercy, He has caused us to be born again to a living hope through the resurrection of Jesus Christ from the dead, to an inheritance that is imperishable, undefiled, and unfading, kept in heaven for you, who by God's power are being guarded through faith for a salvation ready to be revealed in the last time. 1 Peter 1:3–5

The hills teach us to look up; the hills teach us to stand at the top and look out and down. Caves teach us that Christ is the light who guides us from the darkness of the cave into His light and life. Caves teach us that our resurrection will be through the cave. And they teach us to fix our eyes on Christ, our hope and our resurrection.

For individual study, meditate on the following questions. For small-group study, discuss these questions:

1. What have the hills revealed to you through these pages? What have caves revealed to you through these pages?

2. Christ's call to Lazarus to "come forth" is the same as Christ's call to us. What does the call to "come forth" look like in your life?

3. Make a list of the "cave places" in your life. Visualize Christ's words calling you forth; visualize Him stepping out of the cave for you and saying, "Do not fear; trust Me with your life."

4. Make a list of the "hill places" in your life. What causes you to step forth, to look up, to look out?

The view of Half Dome from Glacier Point in Yosemite National Park, California.

High above Lake Tahoe, the author looks to the hills.

Chapter Eight

MOUNTAINS

The rolling hills of central California are flanked by the Sierra Nevada Mountain Range to the east and the Coastal Range to the west. The Coastal Range is more than eight hundred miles long, from north to south. The Sierra Nevada Mountains are over five hundred miles long and seventy miles wide. The highest peak is Mount Whitney. At 14,491 feet above sea level, it is only eighty-five miles from the lowest point in the United States, Death Valley, California, which is 282 feet below sea level.

While California may be best known for cities and beaches, the mountains are spectacular. Mountain sports include backpacking, camping, mountain and rock climbing, snow skiing, and snowboarding. Water sports, such as fishing, white-water rafting, and river floating, are also popular. Nature enthusiasts discover a variety of animals, birds, and flowers unique to the higher altitudes. Some multisport athletes ski the mountains of California in the morning, then drive to the coast and surf in the afternoon.

I have a couple of distinct childhood memories of time in the mountains. The first is a family vacation in Colorado when Dad parked our Ford pickup at the top of Pikes Peak (14,115-foot elevation). While the others were appreciating the spectacular view from the top of the mountain, I had only one mission in mind: to use the bathroom. I ran to the bathroom, only to discover that I needed a dime to open the stall! I rushed back to my parents and begged for a coin; running on top of the mountain in the thin air of the high elevation left me breathless. Only after using the restroom could I enjoy the spectacular scenery in Colorado.

Climbing Half Dome in Yosemite National Park is another great mountain memory. Half Dome is one of the most photographed mountains in the world. Whether taken from across the valley from Glacier Point or from the valley floor (both easily accessible by car), the photos are spectacular. Tourists from around the world come here to take in the view and to take photos from these famous spots. Photos from the opposite direction, on the other hand—the top of Half Dome—are a rarity.

Glacier Point and the valley floor are a relatively short distance from Half Dome as the crow flies, but the 19-mile hike to the 8,800-foot peak, 4,800 feet above the valley floor, is another story! Relatively few have the amazing opportunity to take photos from the top of Half Dome. I had that opportunity on September 11, 2010.

The day hike was grueling but well worth it, and I still relish the accomplishment. As we set out, Half Dome looked so close; but there were times during our trek when it was not even visible from the John Muir Trail. There were also times when we knew we were getting closer, but Half Dome looked so far away. Arriving at the cables that would guide us to the top was exhilarating. Yet the physical challenge of climbing up was only half the journey—I would need to make the descent as well. After seriously considering the journey, I chose to go up—and wow! The view was breathtaking, scary, stunning!

I rested, ate lunch, and thanked God for His awesome creation. I marveled at the magnificent feeling of conquering Half Dome. I dwelt on the fact that the views from the mountain trails are vastly different from the view at the top of the mountain. My photos from the top of Half Dome can't do justice to the handiwork of God.

Mountaintops are so distinctive, so breathtaking, that they inspire the familiar expression "mountaintop experience," which is used to describe a superlative event. What are the mountaintop experiences in your life? In my life, I think of youth group experiences, adult retreats, championship ballgames, the births of my children, my children's weddings, conversations, and successes.

Mountaintop experiences generally bring a sense of awe and wonder. Mountaintop experiences, because of the adrenaline rush, may also bring

A view of the Hecht Hetchy Reservoir in Yosemite National Park.

a desire to stay there, to remain in the moment. Then reality sets in and we acknowledge that although the mountaintop is wonderful, but eventually we must descend back into the "real world." Life milestones, relationships, and spirituality bring mountaintop experiences, and we long for highs if we are bored with—or perhaps even despise—the routine. We let ourselves believe that "there must be more to life" when, realistically, the "more" we seek isn't found only in mountaintop experiences.

Life may also bring events and experiences that feel like insurmountable, unclimbable mountains. We might feel stuck at the foot of the mountain, looking up from the valley or desert of despair. We may want to go around, turn back from, flee from, or ignore the mountain in front of us. We may try everything to avoid the steep, rocky, challenging path in front of us. We don't feel strong enough, courageous enough, smart enough to climb the mountain.

Exploration of the Scriptures about mountains is the basis for this chapter as we continue to uncover God's word and work for us and in us and through us. The life God gave us and continues to give us is alive in Christ through our everyday life, which may take the form of mountaintop experiences or the mountains of challenge. The Rock Speaks through mountains here (wherever "here" is).

Moses' Mountaintop Experiences

Our childhood Sunday School days taught us the stories of the patriarch Moses, yet those great Bible stories include so much more than the simplified versions we may have learned as children. Journeying deeper into the biblical accounts of Moses will help us hear how *The Rock Speaks* through the mountains in Moses' life. Through his stories, God calls to us to see Jesus, the Rock in whom Moses placed his trust.

Moses met God in a burning bush at the foot of Mount Horeb, known also as Mount Sinai and "the mountain of God." His encounter with God at the mountain of God changed his life's path from shepherd of flocks and herds to shepherd of the children of Israel (which some scholars say numbered as many as 2.5 million). Moses resisted; Moses argued with God about his desire to resist God's call; Moses wanted to flee because he was afraid. Please take time to meditate on Exodus 1–4 in their entirety, as only select sections are summarized or printed here.

God spoke from the burning bush, and Moses answered, "Here I am," and took his sandals off at God's request (Exodus 3:1–5). "God said, 'I am the God of your father, the God of Abraham, the God of Isaac, and the God of Jacob.' And Moses hid his face, for he was afraid to look at God" (Exodus 3:6). This extraordinary mountaintop, burning bush experience between God and Moses did not take place in a vacuum.

Moses was born to an Israelite woman, but from infancy he lived in the home of the pharaoh's daughter, an Egyptian, who found him in a basket floating in the Nile River. She named him Moses, which means, "I drew him out of the water." Moses knew his Hebrew heritage. After he had grown up, he stood up to protect a fellow Hebrew by killing an Egyptian. Moses thought there were no witnesses, but word reached the pharaoh that Moses had defended a Hebrew, so he fled to Midian to avoid punishment for his crime: death. There, Moses stood up again to protect people, this time women at a well. This very brief summary of Moses' life from birth to adulthood is recorded in Exodus 2.

Moses' burning bush experience at the foot of God's mountain was the culmination of his life experiences up to that point. God had equipped him through his life experiences for the work He placed in front of him. Through the burning bush, God called Moses to trust, to speak, and to lead. Yet Moses resisted. He didn't believe he could be a leader of God's people because his previous attempts at leadership had not gone well. In response to Moses' argument, God provided Aaron, Moses' brother, as a teammate to lead the people out of slavery.

> The LORD said to Aaron, "Go into the wilderness to meet Moses." So he went and met him at the mountain of God and kissed him. And Moses told Aaron all the words of the LORD with which He had sent him to speak, and all the signs that He had commanded him to do. Then Moses and Aaron went and gathered together all the elders of the people of Israel. Aaron spoke all the words that the LORD had spoken to Moses and did the signs in the sight of the people. And the people believed; and when they heard that the LORD had visited the people of Israel and that He had seen their affliction, they bowed their heads and worshiped. Exodus 4:27–31

This burning bush experience at the foot of Mount Sinai was one of many opportunities for Moses to trust God while leading the children of Israel. God led Moses back to that mountain, along with the throngs of Israelites who had been freed from slavery. God called Moses up the mountain to receive His instructions:

> Thus you shall say to the house of Jacob, and tell the people of Israel: You yourselves have seen what I did to the Egyptians, and how I bore you on eagles' wings and brought you to Myself. Now therefore, if you will indeed obey My voice and keep My covenant, you shall be My treasured possession among all peoples, for all the earth is Mine; and you shall be to Me a kingdom of priests and a holy nation. These are the words that you shall speak to the people of Israel. Exodus 19:3–6

The "mountain of God" story continues with the commitment of the people to obey all the words God spoke to them:

> Then He said to Moses, "Come up to the LORD, you and Aaron, Nadab, and Abihu, and seventy of the elders of Israel, and worship from afar. Moses alone shall come near to the LORD, but the others shall not come near, and the people shall not come up with him." Moses came and told the people all the words of the LORD and all the rules. And all the people answered with one voice and said, "All the words that the LORD has spoken we will do." And Moses wrote down all the words of the LORD. He rose early in the morning and built an altar at the foot of the mountain, and twelve pillars, according to the twelve tribes of Israel. And he sent young men of the people of Israel, who offered burnt offerings and sacrificed peace offerings of oxen to the LORD. And Moses took half of the blood and put it in basins, and half of the blood he threw against the altar. Then he took the Book of the Covenant and read it in the hearing of the people. And they said, "All that the LORD has spoken we will do, and we will be obedient." And Moses took the blood and threw it on the people and said, "Behold the blood of the covenant that the LORD has made with you in accordance with all these words." Exodus 24:1–8

God faithfully brought the children of Israel out of slavery through Moses and Aaron's leadership. The people's response—"All the words that the LORD has spoken we will do"—are powerful words of commitment, a desire of their hearts to respond to God's work of deliverance in their lives. These are mountaintop words from hearts that were truly thankful.

God's covenant, sealed with the blood of the sacrifice, was a sign of His commitment to the people. God saved, God delivered, and God sealed

His covenant with His people. God's covenant was not made because of their faith in Him or their desire to do all that He spoke. His covenant was made and sealed because God chose, through His infinite love and mercy, to make promises and covenants with the people. This is true for us too! Promise and covenant come first and are not dependent upon our words or work. Obedience and commitment follow God's faithfulness.

Freedom from slavery and the covenant with the people came before Moses' next mountaintop experience. God called Moses back up the mountain, and Moses left Aaron in charge of the people. While Moses and God interacted on the mountain, the people got tired of waiting for Moses to come down the mountain. The people's hearts moved, in a forty-day time frame, from deep commitment to this:

> When the people saw that Moses delayed to come down from the mountain, the people gathered themselves together to Aaron and said to him, "Up, make us gods who shall go before us. As for this Moses, the man who brought us up out of the land of Egypt, we do not know what has become of him." So Aaron said to them, "Take off the rings of gold that are in the ears of your wives, your sons, and your daughters, and bring them to me." So all the people took off the rings of gold that were in their ears and brought them to Aaron. And he received the gold from their hand and fashioned it with a graving tool and made a golden calf. And they said, "These are your gods, O Israel, who brought you up out of the land of Egypt!" When Aaron saw this, he built an altar before it. And Aaron made a proclamation and said, "Tomorrow shall be a feast to the Lord." And they rose up early the next day and offered burnt offerings and brought peace offerings. And the people sat down to eat and drink and rose up to play. Exodus 32:1–6

God's anger burned against the people to the point that He wanted to destroy them. Moses challenged God with His own covenant, his faithfulness delivering the people from the hands of the enemy, and about His promises to Abraham, Isaac, and Jacob. God, rather than destroying the people, worked through Moses to express His anger at their disobedience. As we explored in chapter 4, Moses threw the stone tablets in anger. In this chapter, we focus on the movement of the hearts of the people. They had abandoned their mountaintop commitment to obey every word of God, and instead worshiped an idol crafted from their fine jewelry.

Aaron, the spiritual leader, bowed to the desire of the people and created an idol for them to worship. Aaron's leadership faltered even further when Moses confronted him with the truth; Aaron lied to cover his own disobedience to the word and covenant of God.

> Aaron said, "Let not the anger of my lord burn hot. You know the people, that they are set on evil. For they said to me, 'Make us gods who shall go before us. As for this Moses, the man who brought us up out of the land of Egypt, we do not know what has become of him.' So I said to them, 'Let any who have gold take it off.' So they gave it to me, and I threw it into the fire, and out came this calf."
> Exodus 32:22–24

Moses wasn't immune to faltering either. He went from mountaintop commitment to following his own ways through lack of trust, insecurity, and stubbornness. Here are a few points we learn. Mountaintop experiences are blessings. Mountaintop commitment to God is an important part of our spiritual journey. Having said that, our focus must always begin and end with God's eternal covenant through the blood of Christ, the Rock, who was sacrificed for us. God's faithfulness is our hope. We trust God at His Word, as Moses said in his final words to the people that it was not because of their righteousness or the uprightness of their hearts that they were going to possess life, but because of God's faithfulness to them (see Deuteronomy 9 and 10).

We study these stories from the full view looking back. Moses couldn't have known the end of the story, as he was taking steps each moment of each day by faith. Yet he fixed his eyes on the Promised One, the Messiah, who was not only foretold but also was present in these stories. Like Moses, we cannot see the end of our stories, but the call to trust God with each step we take is clear. We fix our eyes on the Messiah, who has come and is present among us, holding us and journeying with us as we learn to trust.

God's call on our lives doesn't take place in a vacuum. Rather, He calls us to believe that He is at work, guiding us to deeper trust through our stories within the context of our life experiences. We may argue with God about our lack of skills for the call. His answer to us is the same as it was to Moses at God's holy mountain: "Trust Me. I provide. I work through these mountains—and valleys—to bring you and those around you to deeper faith and trust. Keep your eyes fixed on Jesus, My Son."

Jesus' Mountaintop Experiences

Jesus' earthly journey included two mountaintop experiences. One took place with the devil as he tempted Jesus; the other with the disciples and patriarchs, Moses and Elijah. We will explore those two stories, keeping in mind Jesus' declaration, "Truly, I say to you, if you have faith like a grain of mustard seed, you will say to this mountain, 'Move from here to there,' and it will move, and nothing will be impossible for you" (Matthew 17:20).

The Spirit of God led the Son of God into three face-to-face encounters with Satan. Matthew said, "Jesus was led up by the Spirit into the wilderness to be tempted by the devil. And after fasting forty days and forty nights, He was hungry" (Matthew 4:1–2). Jesus' temptation was necessary for the completion of His earthly mission. Adam and Eve failed to resist Satan's temptation, but Jesus did resist and kept the Word of God perfectly for us. Jesus had needs yet chose not to fulfill those needs through Satan's tempting.

The tempter offered Jesus bread, and Jesus replied, "Man shall not live by bread alone, but by every word that comes from the mouth of God" (Matthew 4:4). John records Jesus' words during the encounter with the disciples and the woman at the well: "My food is to do the will of Him who sent Me and to accomplish His work" (John 4:34). Jesus' hunger for food to meet His physical needs and His refusal to give in to temptation directs our attention to the nourishment the Word of God provides. Jesus' singular focus was accomplishing the will and work of God.

Jesus stood up to the tempter's second test on the mountain. Satan invited Jesus to throw Himself down from the pinnacle of the temple and trust the angels to lift Him up. Jesus declared, "You shall not put the Lord your God to the test" (Matthew 4:7; Deuteronomy 6:16). Adam and Eve trusted Satan at his word; Jesus said, "Don't test Me." The Word of God is trustworthy; Jesus' word is trustworthy.

Finally, Satan led Jesus up a high mountain and showed Him all the kingdoms of the world. He demanded that Jesus bow down and worship him. The Son of God faced Satan, the one whose successful temptation of Adam and Eve led God's beautiful, perfect creation into disobedience, punishment, and death. Jesus answered Satan's demand with these powerful words: "Then Jesus said to him, 'Be gone, Satan! For it is written, "You shall worship the Lord your God and Him only shall you serve."' Then the devil left Him, and behold, angels came and were ministering to Him" (Matthew 4:10–11).

Thank God that Jesus denied Satan! Thank God that Jesus lived a perfect life! Through His life, suffering, death, and resurrection, we live life here and now in expectant hope. We worship the risen, living Lord who defeated the tempter when we could not. We cannot imagine the devastation had Jesus worshiped Satan on that high mountain. Faith "sees" a greater picture of freedom and mercy in Christ through Jesus' defeat of sin, death, and the devil.

Jesus' second mountaintop experience took place with three of His disciples. They did not travel alone on this mountaintop journey. Jesus and His disciples met the patriarchs and heard the voice of God for encouragement in the journey to the cross.

> And after six days Jesus took with Him Peter and James, and John his brother, and led them up a high mountain by themselves. And He was transfigured before them, and His face shone like the sun, and His clothes became white as light. And behold, there appeared to them Moses and Elijah, talking with Him. And Peter said to Jesus, "Lord, it is good that we are here. If You wish, I will make three tents here, one for You and one for Moses and one for Elijah." He was still speaking when, behold, a bright cloud overshadowed them, and a voice from the cloud said, "This is My beloved Son, with whom I am well pleased; listen to Him." When the disciples heard this, they fell on their faces and were terrified. But Jesus came and touched them, saying, "Rise, and have no fear." And when they lifted up their eyes, they saw no one but Jesus only. And as they were coming down the mountain, Jesus commanded them, "Tell no one the vision, until the Son of Man is raised from the dead." Matthew 17:1–9

God reveals His heart through this mountaintop story in numerous ways. God's love for His Son is expressed by providing Moses and Elijah to talk with Jesus. The loneliness of His journey to the cross was eased by the encouraging conversation with faithful men who had seen and proclaimed the Messiah in their day. Luke records this detail of the conversation: "And behold, two men were talking with Him, Moses and Elijah, who appeared in glory and spoke of His departure, which He was about to accomplish at Jerusalem" (Luke 9:30–31).

God's love for the disciples was revealed as He allowed them to witness Jesus' divinity through the transfiguration. The disciples were also given the gift of hearing the voice of God. God's heart is revealed as He interrupted Peter's voice, thoughtful as he was when he suggested putting up tents where they were on the mountain. The disciples were terrified! They were accustomed to Peter's voice, but this was the very voice of God, which affirmed Jesus' Sonship and said, "Listen to Him." Terrified and falling facedown to the ground was the only response to God's voice in the presence of His Son and the patriarchs.

God's love in Jesus was revealed in His words "Rise, and have no fear." We are called to humbly receive, to be quiet and listen. We are called to be in awe that God provided Moses and Elijah to Jesus for profound conversation and encouragement. We are called to learn that building monuments to our mountaintop experiences is not God-pleasing. Our tendency is to run down the mountain and shout out our experiences. Instead, we are to heed Jesus' word to keep mountaintop experiences between us and Him for a time to ponder them in our own heart, to cherish and discern the experiences. After a time, we can relay the stories of our mountaintop experiences.

Mountaintop Experiences Today

Mountaintop experiences take place within the context of daily life. Individuals, even siblings and identical twins, have a life path that is unique to them, and they will experience mountaintop highs differently. Our thoughts discerning our experiences are also unique, based in our life experiences and the culture in which we were raised. Discerning experiences properly leads to embracing and nourishing our uniqueness as part of God's call on our lives. In addition to our mountaintop highs, our daily routines and valleys need discernment according to the Word of God.

Jesus guided the three disciples' discernment of the mountain of transfiguration. He didn't entertain Peter's suggestion to build three tents in honor of Jesus, Moses, and Elijah. He touched them to raise them up from terror into His peace and presence. He also guided them not to tell anyone about the experience. Finally, as they asked questions, Jesus revealed more about His impending journey to the cross. They, like Moses, journeyed one step at a time in faith in the Messiah's redemptive work.

We know these stories so well, but have we placed ourselves into these stories? Do we believe that Jesus successfully faced temptation for *us*? Do we allow Jesus to journey with us on the mountains, in the valleys? Do we discern our life events from within the context of the Word of God?

Just as the disciples were continually challenged to think differently by the very Word of God in their midst, so are we. Jesus touches us and says, "Rise up and have no fear." Jesus says, "Live life in Me, and follow Me."

Mountaintop experiences often lead people to make the bold faith statement "All God says, we will do" (see Exodus 24). Yet, as we've explored, within days of that declaration, the free people of Israel, with their leader's help, were worshiping an idol they had built. It is easy to worship mountaintop (and valley) experiences; it is easy to worship the church building or our heritage or even our thoughts. Jesus calls us to rise up in faith, to worship Him alone in spirit and in truth. Jesus calls us to embrace the journey with Him in faith and trust.

Our thinking, discernment, and faith are challenged when we place ourselves into interactions between Jesus and His disciples. We are challenged, for example, by these words of Jesus: "For truly, I say to you, if you have faith like a grain of mustard seed, you will say to this mountain, 'Move from here to there,' and it will move, and nothing will be impossible for you" (Matthew 17:20). And "Truly, I say to you, if you have faith and do not doubt, you will not only do what has been done to the fig tree, but even if you say to this mountain, 'Be taken up and thrown into the sea,' it will happen. And whatever you ask in prayer, you will receive, if you have faith" (Matthew 21:21–22).

Judge William P. Clark, Secretary of the Interior in the Ronald Reagan administration, built this mission-style chapel atop a hill near Shandon, California.

We may be tempted to set aside these encounters because Jesus was talking to His disciples, not to us. But there is trouble in doing so because then we would need to comb through the Gospels to discern which words were meant for the disciples only and which are for us. Matthew recorded these words for us to challenge us in the context of our lives right here, right now. Our Lord knows that we are afraid to ask, "Which mountains in my life need to be moved?" Nevertheless, He raises us up and says, "I am with you; I am for you." Here is a short list of mountains that may need to be moved. Perhaps you have other mountains to add to this list.

- Thoughts of being unworthy, based in the inability to truly hear and discern Christ's mercy "for *me*." It is true that on our own, we are not worthy to receive God's grace; however, we are worth Christ's sacrifice simply because God calls us to be His own and gives us His love and mercy.

- Comparing ourselves to others and judging ourselves to be better or less than.

- Pride or arrogance when a mountain we've faced has been moved as though we, rather than God, moved it.

- Taking care of, feeding, and nourishing our entire being—body, soul, heart, spirit, emotions, mind, and senses.

- The isolation caused by feeling that we're the only one struggling in our faith walk and by the lack of opportunity to engage in profound conversations with others who will cherish our story.

- Loneliness, fear, hard-heartedness, anger, resentment, jealousy, envy, strife.

- Pretending and pretense.

Immediately after their mountaintop experience, Jesus sent out His disciples to heal people in His name. The disciples' journey didn't begin with declaring that they would move mountains. The disciples healed all but one—a boy with a demon. When they questioned why they couldn't heal that one person, Jesus called them "men of little faith" and went on to tell them about "faith to move mountains" (see Matthew 17).

The disciples were limited by lack of faith and by fear. We are limited by the same things. Jesus' word and work take us beyond any self-imposed or other-imposed limits. Jesus' word and work are not limited; He is the mountain mover and He works mountain moving for us, in us, and through us.

Still, mountain-moving faith declaration can be taken to an unhealthy extreme, as when families deny medical attention to loved ones in the name of faith, when they believe that if they pray enough and believe enough, the family member will be healed. In some cases, God works healing in an immediate, miraculous way. In other cases, God works through the hands of physicians. In other cases, God calls a loved one to Himself. Perhaps a mountain that needs to be moved is a heart that sees the possibility of God's work in only one way.

God has moved mountains in my life. With support from family and friends, one mountain that was moved was that I began to learn and believe that God wanted me alive, to live and breathe in a healthy home. I had lived in fear in a home filled with domestic violence. I was blind to the pain I experienced during my marriage, living in a constant state of trying to make myself better so explosions wouldn't happen. I believed divorce was wrong and that I would be a terrible failure if I chose to care for myself. I believed no one would believe me or love me if I spoke the truth of my life and existence. I prayed for peace in my home with no hope of that ever happening. Finally, I said "stop" and asked my husband to leave our home for a time of separation so we could get help. I initiated the divorce process when I discerned that I couldn't live in my marriage in safety and peace.

Another mountain that moved was the change in my heart. I had been taught that if I just had enough faith, therapy wouldn't be necessary. Seeking professional help took a lot of courage. I sought therapy and grew tremendously through it—and another mountain slowly moved. The mountains of unhealthy shame are moving slowly too. Another mountain that has been moving is the slow process of my heart healing, embracing living, and learning to live a single life.

Your story and mine are as unique as you and I are. Identifying mountains and asking Jesus for discernment, courage, and wisdom are important steps in the journey of faith. Asking Jesus for guidance and faith is also important mountain climbing, mountain moving. Asking trusted people for help with discernment and wisdom is important too.

In addition to the mountains in our personal lives that need to be moved, God also calls us to carefully and lovingly discern the mountains of religion in our Western culture that need to be moved. Have many modern-day religious leaders turned into the Pharisees, Scribes, Sadducees—those I call "religious leaders" of the Scriptures? Do these modern-day leaders know all the right answers in their heads but have no heart for the broken and the lost? Here are a few mountains I see; think about this list and prayerfully, carefully add to it. Please use the Scriptures' great love and discernment so that we don't become mountains ourselves!

- Thinking others need to think like us or act like us in order to embrace faith in Christ.

- Lip service but not hearts of mercy to the hurting and broken.

- Believing "worship" takes place only within the walls of a building (see John 4:19–26; John 9:35–38; Romans 12:1).[6]

- Building monuments to our heritage and or worshiping our heritage rather than the Christ (see Matthew 17).[7]

- Religious leaders may have knowledge or faith to move a mountain, but without love it is nothing (see 1 Corinthians 13:2).

While He walked on this earth, Jesus called people to Himself, to a journey of life in His holy life and growth as His holy people. Moving mountains through faith in Him was part of the call. That call was not easy to follow or simple to carry out, but Jesus provided everything His followers needed. He provided for them, and He provides for us to fulfill His call today. The work and Word of God breed life, cause faith to grow in our hearts, and provide courage to follow Christ's call. Christ's obedience is our hope; our obedience and praise are our grateful response.

Mountains remind us that our Creator cares for us. God worked through Mount Sinai to call Moses, to make a covenant with His people, and to provide the Ten Commandments, which express His heart for His people. God worked through the mountain of temptation that Jesus faced as well as through the mountain of transfiguration where the authority of the Messiah was declared. God works through the mountains we face to draw us closer to Him. Mountains teach us that there is hope, always, in Christ, both now and for eternity.

---

6 The importance of gathering with others to confess our need for our Savior, receive forgiveness, hear the Word of God proclaimed, celebrate our Baptism into Christ's family, and feast on the Lord's Supper is not undermined by this statement. I praise God for the opportunity to gather around Word and Sacrament as one aspect of the ebb and flow of our Christian life.
7 Theology and tradition are beautiful, not for the sake of theology and tradition, but only for the Christ they lift up.

For individual study, meditate on the following questions. For small-group study, discuss these questions:

1. What have the mountains revealed to you through these pages?

2. Reflect on a mountaintop experience.

3. Identify mountains in your life that need to be moved. Ask for wisdom and discernment. Pray for trusted people to journey with you.

4. Meditate on Moses' words in Psalm 90:1–4: "Lord, You have been our dwelling place in all generations. Before the mountains were brought forth, or ever You had formed the earth and the world, from everlasting to everlasting You are God. You return man to dust and say, 'Return, O children of man!' For a thousand years in Your sight are but as yesterday when it is past, or as a watch in the night."

A Jeep ride through Steinbeck Vineyards provides countless photo opportunities.

Chapter Nine

THE LAND

My ancestors packed their belongings into trunks and boarded a ship heading toward a new land—America—in the 1860s. They settled in Geneseo, Illinois, for a short time and then moved west to California in 1884. They named their new community Geneseo. It is very near the booming little city of Paso Robles, halfway between San Francisco and Los Angeles. The new land called these pioneering families through a newspaper article that read, "Good farmland, cheap, and we're looking for families to help us start a Lutheran Church."

Christmas Eve 2014 marked the 130th year of our family living off the land. The land in our community continues to call my family members. Six generations have answered the call; my grandchildren are the seventh. My father has lived off this land for most of his life. My brother and I were called home after careers in professional ministry, my brother as a pastor, and I as a family life minister. For his entire life, my son has felt the call to work the land and the deep desire to work with his grandpa. We are three generations working together.

This ancient oak grows atop Grandma's Hill at Steinbeck Vineyards.

Living off the land is not without challenges. I've heard stories of children who didn't fit the farmer mold being forced to farm or being ostracized because they wouldn't. Farming carries tremendous challenges because of nature and economics. Crops can be devastated by lack of rain or flooding or frost. There were years that crop prices dropped so low that the family had to sell a portion of the land to pay bills.

Living off the land is not a nine-to-five job. When work needs to get done, we work until the work is done. We rest during the seasons of the year that are slower. We travel on vacations during those months, making sure that a family member is always present at home to oversee operations.

My parents, my brother's family, and I live in homes built on land that our family owns, and so the inheritance that is passed from family member to family member includes our dwelling places. We've learned,

through the generations, that living off the land and caring for all things on the land must be a passion. If living off the land is not in the blood of the inheritor, the legacy will end with the sale or loss of the land. We've taken great care to pass along the inheritance based on the family member's desire to live off the land.

My son wanted to work with his grandpa from the day he was old enough to comprehend what his grandpa did. Tractors, farm equipment, and soil were his passion when he was growing up. His work ethic and passion mirror my dad's love for the land. One day during his teen years, as my son and I were working on a project together, he said, "Mom, don't forget Grandpa built this [business, vineyard, etc.]!" My heart melted, and I promised that I would never forget nor take for granted what Dad built for us to work and enjoy.

Protecting the land is part of our culture. There have been and always will be forces attacking property ownership. Today we fight the battle of maintaining our right to use the water under our land. The future will bring a different battle. We fight from the heart with all our might because of our passion for the land and the privilege of living off the land.

Stewardship of the land is our culture, too, as we value our natural resources. We are stewards, caretakers. We farm sustainably, safely, and never wastefully so the generations that follow can enjoy living off the land. We know that ultimately, everything we possess is a gift from God and that He provides the opportunity for the work of our hands to express our heart and passion for the land.

Living off the land provides a lens through which I see the Old Testament promises of God through the inheritance. Exploring through that lens opens up further opportunity to grasp the gifts God has for us. The promises, spoken and gifted many times to many people, foreshadowed Christ's work on the land and the gift of an eternal land. People of all times have journeyed on and lived off the land. Embracing God's work and God's promises of a greater inheritance is the call of the Scriptures through the land.

THE PROMISED LAND: THE JOURNEY BEGINS

Adam was placed into a type of promised land when God put Him into the Garden of Eden. God placed Adam there, as we discussed in chapter 1, to care for God's creation and to live in relationship with his Creator and with his wife. Their promised land was perfect in every way until Adam and Eve chose to disobey the one and only command God had set before them. Their rest, as well as the harmony and the perfection of the land of promise, was immediately and irrevocably lost.

Punishment came. God removed Adam and Eve from the land of perfection. He spoke punishment to Adam, Eve, and the serpent. The land would no longer yield only bountiful blessings; it would also yield weeds. Weeds would challenge Adam's hands, and living off the land would be painful. Childbearing would be painful. The serpent would crawl on his belly. God's punishment came through His word, the very word spoken to create. God's punishment placed upon them things they could not possibly understand. Adam had never pulled a weed, Eve had never given birth, and the serpent had not crawled on his belly.

The curse of death as punishment also came through the Word of God. Adam would return to the dust from which he had been taken. Death became an eventuality of the punishment God declared on them. God had not created Adam and Eve for death; He created them for living. Returning to dust through dying and death was completely unknown to them. They had never suffered or died. When they heard these words coupled with the other punishments they heard, they must have been overwhelmed. The only actual punishments they were living with in that very moment were removal from the garden land and God's harsh words.

Adam and Eve's sin led to brokeness. That brokenness was manifested through hiding, lying, and covering their nakedness. Adam and Eve experienced brokenness with each other. They blamed each other; they hid from God, lied to Him, and even blamed Him. We inherited the guilt of Adam and Eve's original sin, and we have inherited their punishments. We have also inherited the unhealthy blame and shame, which were manifested immediately after they disobeyed God's command. God's punishment and all of the challenges of living life as sinful human beings are our inheritance, and this is distinctly tied to the land.

Promise came too. The serpent would be crushed by an offspring of Adam and Eve, the One who would be greater. We know that Jesus is the

Promised One, but Adam and Eve didn't know that. Eve thought her first son, Cain, was the fulfillment of that promise. We look back at times to the good old days. Imagine Adam and Eve discussing their days in the garden after a long day farming the land, in pain from pulling the weeds or in pain from childbirth.

In faith, Adam and Eve clung to the Word of God, the promise of God. Removal from their first Promised Land was the punishment; dying and death was the punishment. Their eventual death was a stepping stone God provided for entrance into their final Promised Land, face-to-face with their Creator for eternity. In faith, we cling to the Word of God and the promises of God. Understanding our relationship to the land and to Adam and Eve helps to increase our faith in God and in His Son, the fulfillment of God's promises. We may, in our youth, have the ability to ignore the inheritance we have received from Adam and Eve, our eventual return to the dust. In our youth, we may also fail to hear the word of life for us. As we experience life and as we witness death, we are called to ponder God's promises more fully.

Wrestling with faith in God's promises is not unique to us; people of all time have wrestled with the faith journey. Scripture provides many examples of the faith journey. In this chapter, we will briefly explore the journey of four patriarchs of the faith—Abraham, Joseph, Moses, and Joshua—to the Promised Land.

The Promised Land: The Journey of Faith through Abraham's Story

Two thousand years after God's promise to Adam and Eve (only nine chapters in Genesis), Abram was directed to leave his homeland. As he followed God's call, God promised a land to Abram. Two thousand years is one hundred generations, a very long time to wait for another promise from God! Abram was given a promise—a gift of the land to hand down to his offspring—but he was seventy-five years old and had no children.

> Then the LORD appeared to Abram and said, "To your off-spring I will give this land." So he built there an altar to the LORD, who had appeared to him. From there he moved to the hill country on the east of Bethel and pitched his tent, with Bethel on the west and Ai on the east. And there he built an altar to the LORD and called upon the name of the LORD. And Abram journeyed on, still going toward the Negeb. Now there was a famine in the land. So Abram went down to Egypt to sojourn there, for the famine was severe in the land. Genesis 12:7–10

> The LORD said to Abram, after Lot had separated from him, "Lift up your eyes and look from the place where you are, northward and southward and eastward and westward, for all the land that you see I will give to you and to your offspring forever. I will make your offspring as the dust of the earth, so that if one can count the dust of the earth, your offspring also can be counted. Arise, walk through the length and the breadth of the land, for I will give it to you." Genesis 13:14–17

These promises from God to Abram were tied to the land and to his offspring, which foreshadowed an eternal land, a heavenly home, and the children of the promise. Abram lived as a sojourner, a temporary dweller, both in Egypt and in his own land as he looked forward to the Promised Land. God also foretold that Abram's offspring would be sojourners and servants in a foreign land for four hundred years (Genesis 15:13), which would lead to deliverance into the Promised Land.

Years later, God's promise to Isaac affirmed the promise He had made to Abraham, his father. Isaac was also called to be a sojourner in the land

of promise. He was also called to live the inheritance, with all of its blessings, while keeping the promises of God for an eternal land in heart and mind. God promised:

> Sojourn in this land, and I will be with you and will bless you, for to you and to your offspring I will give all these lands, and I will establish the oath that I swore to Abraham your father. I will multiply your offspring as the stars of heaven and will give to your offspring all these lands. And in your offspring all the nations of the earth shall be blessed, because Abraham obeyed My voice and kept My charge, My commandments, My statutes, and My laws. Genesis 26:3–5

The gift of the land carried with it the responsibility of taking care of the land and taking care to obey God's voice, His commands, and laws.

Dwelling in the land and sojourning on the land was a gift as well as a responsibility to live fully as children of the living God, children of a grand promise.

The Promised Land: The Journey of Faith through Joseph's Story

In Joseph's story, God worked through the land upon which He placed mankind to sojourn and dwell. Joseph's father, Jacob, had twelve sons by four wives. His wife Rachel gave birth to Joseph and Benjamin. As Joseph grew, his brothers were jealous of him and sold him to traders who were traveling through Canaan to Egypt to sell their goods. When they arrived in Egypt, the tradesmen sold Joseph as a slave, and eventually Joseph rose to power in this foreign land because of his ability to interpret dreams, particularly the dreams of the pharaoh.

Famine forced Joseph's brothers to leave Canaan and journey to Egypt to buy food. Joseph recognized his brothers and had mercy on them. Through sojourning in the foreign land, Joseph saved his family, and God worked through the land to bring about His promises. Joseph instructed his brothers to tell the pharaoh that their occupation was shepherds of the herds. Scripture states that shepherds were an abomination to Egyptians (Genesis 46:34). Shepherds were lowly and humble in all societies, but to Egyptians they were a disgrace, an anathema.

Pharaoh happily assigned Joseph's brothers the task of caring for the flocks and herds. He gave them their own land for their families and flocks. Through the land in Egypt and through shepherds, God's promises were carried out. That which was an anathema to some was grace-filled by God for salvation to others. This story is a forward-looking picture of the Good Shepherd, Jesus, an anathema to some but the very grace of God through His life, death, and resurrection for children of the promise.

Jacob (Israel) spoke these words to his son as he was dying:

> The God before whom my fathers Abraham and Isaac walked, the God who has been my shepherd all my life long to this day, the angel who has redeemed me from all evil, bless the boys; and in them let my name be carried on, and the name of my fathers Abraham and Isaac; and let them grow into a multitude in the midst of the earth. Genesis 48:15–16

Joseph's brothers worried that after their father died, Joseph would take away their land and destroy them. They begged Joseph, at their father's request, to forgive them. Joseph's grace-filled words and emotion touch our hearts today. They give us both guidance and courage to forgive those who have wounded us in our journey on the land.

But Joseph said to them, "Do not fear, for am I in the place of God? As for you, you meant evil against me, but God meant it for good, to bring it about that many people should be kept alive, as they are today. So do not fear; I will provide for you and your little ones." Thus he comforted them and spoke kindly to them. Genesis 50:19–21

The Promised Land: The Journey Continues through Moses and Joshua

Hundreds of years later, God raised up Moses to shepherd the children of Israel, now a grand nation living in slavery in the land of Egypt. These verses reveal God's continued mercy in providing freedom from slavery and deliverance into the land promised to Abraham, Isaac, and Jacob:

God spoke to Moses and said to him, "I am the LORD. I appeared to Abraham, to Isaac, and to Jacob, as God Almighty, but by My name the LORD I did not make Myself known to them. I also established My covenant with them to give them the land of Canaan, the land in which they lived as sojourners. Moreover, I have heard the groaning of the people of Israel whom the Egyptians hold as slaves, and I have remembered My covenant. Say therefore to the people of Israel, 'I am the Lord, and I will bring you out from under the burdens of the Egyptians, and I will deliver you from slavery to them, and I will redeem you with an outstretched arm and with great acts of judgment. I will take you to be My people, and I will be your God, and you shall know that I am the LORD your God, who has brought you out from under the burdens of the Egyptians. I will bring you into the land that I swore to give to Abraham, to Isaac, and to Jacob. I will give it to you for a possession. I am the LORD." Exodus 6:2–8

Moses was called by God to lead the children of Israel out of the land in which they were slaves and into the land of promise and freedom. The children of Israel wandered as sojourners in the desert for forty years! That desert land should have taken only a few weeks to cross! The journey provided many opportunities for the people to trust God through Moses' leadership. We learn through the stories of God's justice and mercy.

Moses' passage through the desert land to his final promised land took strength and courage. He faced the fact that he would not enter into the land promised with the children of Israel; yet, by dying, he entered into the eternal land prepared by God for him. We learn from Moses' experiences that we, too, live this incredible tension. We desire rest in our homeland; we desire rest in our eternal land. Strength and courage are necessary to fully live in our homeland; strength and courage are necessary to journey to our eternal land. Living in rest here is practice for dying to live eternally. Dying, we live in rest, fully in the promised land of complete rest.

Joshua received God's call to lead amid this tension too. These are Joshua's words just before entering the Promised Land:

> "Have I not commanded you? Be strong and courageous. Do not be frightened, and do not be dismayed, for the LORD your God is with you wherever you go." And Joshua commanded the officers of the people, "Pass through the midst of the camp and command the people, 'Prepare your provisions, for within three days you are to pass over this Jordan to go in to take possession of the land that the LORD your God is giving you to possess.'" And to the Reubenites, the Gadites, and the half-tribe of Manasseh Joshua said, "Remember the word that Moses the servant of the LORD commanded you, saying, 'The LORD your God is providing you a place of rest and will give you this land.'"
> Joshua 1:9–13

The land into which the children of Israel were entering, God stated, would be a place of rest. Joshua's words of promise have this same tension. He called the people to be strong and courageous to enter into the land of rest. These weary sojourners would need strength and courage because of the perils they would face; they would need to have faith and trust that God was with them wherever they went. Rest was promised through the land; strength and courage were demanded for the journey.

Rest in the Promised Land was gifted by God, along with strength and courage. Our journey in the land of rest is now, in Christ, our true rest, with knowledge of one day entering the promised land fully. Today, as well as the day we pass through this life and enter the land of rest, takes tremendous strength and courage! God equips us and calls us to more trust, more strength, and more courage in the journey. This journey is filled with healthy tension. We fully rest in Christ today. Christ grants strength and

The picturesque Colorado River in Dead Horse Point State Park in Utah.

courage necessary for the journey in this land and the strength and courage necessary for passing into our eternal promised land.

God's Promises Fulfilled: Jesus' Journey on the Land

The promises of God fulfilled for Adam and Eve, Abraham, Moses, and Joshua foreshadowed Christ's entrance into this world through Mary and Joseph. Our Creator humbled Himself and became a sojourner in the land in order to fulfill the promises God made to the patriarchs. Joseph and Mary, who was with child, journeyed from their homeland to Bethlehem, where the Christ was born and the promise fulfilled. Lowly shepherds celebrated the birth of the Good Shepherd.

Parents and child journeyed from Bethlehem to the land of Egypt. Matthew records, "And he [Joseph] rose and took the child and His mother by night and departed to Egypt and remained there until the death of Herod. This was to fulfill what the Lord had spoken by the prophet, 'Out of Egypt I called My son'" (Matthew 2:14–15). When political conditions were safe, at the call of the angel, the family's journey continued out of Egypt to Nazareth. Matthew recorded:

> When Herod died, behold, an angel of the Lord appeared in a dream to Joseph in Egypt, saying, "Rise, take the child and His mother and go to the land of Israel, for those who sought the child's life are dead." And he rose and took the child and His mother and went to the land of Israel. But when he heard that Archelaus was reigning over Judea in place of his father Herod, he was afraid to go there, and being warned in a dream he withdrew to the district of Galilee. And he went and lived in a city called Nazareth, so that what was spoken by the prophets might be fulfilled, that He would be called a Nazarene. Matthew 2:19–23

Jesus' earthly ministry began in the land called "the wilderness of Judea" at the Jordan River, where John baptized Him in a specific place on the land. The Son of God became flesh to dwell among us at a specific time and in a specific place. He dwelled on the land as a sojourner, a foreigner. He wasn't at home, and His journey on the land was a life on the move. Zigzagging throughout the Promised Land, Jesus proclaimed Himself the fulfillment of all God's promises in and through His life.

Jesus' proclamation included words and actions that called people to Himself. His life—His flesh—was and is rest, an eternal dwelling place. In faith, people flocked to Him and clung to Him. The call to strength and courage rang loud and clear as Jesus called followers. In addition to the call, Jesus provided them with everything they needed to fulfill His call as they journeyed with Him, in Him, on the land.

Jesus' proclamation also created hatred, deep unrest, and utter disgust, as religious leaders saw Him as an anathema to God's promises. The Good Shepherd knew that murderous hearts would respond to His Word by taking action against Him. The promises of God were fulfilled as our sojourning Savior gave Himself over to suffering and death on the cross. Jesus stated the necessity of this aspect of His journey, declaring it the precise purpose for which He had been born when His disciples tried to help Him avoid suffering and death (John 12:27).

Jesus' resurrection sealed the promises of God in the life of Christ, showing us that the land was simply a temporary grave that could not hold Him. By faith, we cling to Christ as our rest; by faith, we see Him as our dwelling place; by faith, we view ourselves as sojourners in this land, but completely at home and at rest in the life of Christ. The author of Hebrews stated, "For if Joshua had given them rest, God would not have spoken of another day later on. So then, there remains a Sabbath rest for the people of God, for whoever has entered God's rest has also rested from his works as God did from His" (Hebrews 4:8–10).

Christ is the completion of the rest of which Joshua spoke. Christ is the fulfillment of all of the promises of God, including eternity. Jesus said, "Today this Scripture has been fulfilled in your hearing" (Luke 4:21), and, "I am the resurrection and the life" (John 11:25). Living eternity in rest means living our inheritance of the promised land now, within the context of abiding in Christ, while dwelling in the land.

The image of life and rest in Christ comes alive through the process of grafting one grape varietal into another vine, a host home. Grafting is performed in the nurseries on very young grapevines, called rootstock. Rootstock does not bear fruit but is the host home for the varietal, such as Cabernet Sauvignon. A deep, V-shaped slice is made in the wood of the trunk of the rootstock just above the soil line. A tiny bud is cut away from a live Cabernet branch to match the V-shaped cut in the trunk. The bud is quickly placed into the flesh of the trunk and a Band-Aid-like substance is tied around the bleeding wounds. Each bleeds sap, and the two grow together into vine and branch.[8]

The rootstock is "the vine" for the thirty- to fifty-year life of the plant; the bud becomes the branch; that branch becomes the trunk, and eventually branches grow and are trained on the wires and produce fruit. Rootstock is used as a home for the varietal because rootstock is resistant to disease, drought, and salt. It matches our particular soils and climate. The scar on the trunk is always visible and grows with the plant. The scar is the place through which the energy of the vine flows.

Christ, the Root of David, is our Rootstock.[9] He is not susceptible to sin or death. Christ is our home. Paul used this imagery of grafting and concluded, "If the root is holy, so are the branches" (Romans 11:16). Christ

---

8   I explore the art of grafting and connect the imagery to Old Testament promises fulfilled in Christ in great detail in my book *The Vine Speaks* (St. Louis: Concordia Publishing House, 2013).

9   Isaiah 11:1, 10; Revelation 5:5; 22:16

is our resting place wherever we are and whatever land we dwell in. Christ is eternal, and life abiding in Christ is eternal. We live in Christ today, the very same place we will dwell for all eternity.

Peter declared, "He himself bore our sins in His body on the tree, that we might die to sin and live to righteousness. By His wounds you have been healed" (1 Peter 2:24). Peter's healing words draw our attention to the grapevine's wounds and healing during the grafting and growing processes. The vine and the branch become one through sap flow and healing. Both vine and branch grow within the solid, healed relationship. Sap, the lifeblood of the vine, flows through the healed wound. The apostles use the phrase "in Christ" more than one hundred times in the Epistles as they invite us to grasp and believe the relationship Christ established for us, that is, dwelling in His holy life. "By His wounds you have been healed!" Peter's words quoted the prophet Isaiah. These powerful words are spoken in this context:

> You are a chosen race, a royal priesthood, a holy nation, a people for His own possession, that you may proclaim the excellencies of Him who called you out of darkness into His marvelous light. Once you were not a people, but now you are God's people; once you had not received mercy, but now you have received mercy. Beloved, I urge you as sojourners and exiles to abstain from the passions of the flesh, which wage war against your soul. 1 Peter 2:9–11

As healed members of the Body of Christ, we are called to live as precious, holy sojourners in the land. Recall also, from the same chapter, that Peter calls us living stones of the Chief Cornerstone. We live in Christ, in faith, through Baptism into His holy life, our home. We sojourn in this land grafted into Christ's life now and for eternity.

THE PROMISED LAND: LIVING THE PROMISE, ETERNITY IN CHRIST TODAY ON THE LAND

God's promises have been fulfilled in Christ, and through the relationship Christ established for us, we live eternally today and forever. Like it was for the patriarchs, the promised land is ours long before we enter it. The patriarchs lived the promise and inheritance by faith before receiving it fully. We learn from them to fix our eyes on the fulfilled promises as well as on the future completion of the promises. As sojourners, the patriarchs lived life on the land; as sojourners, we live life on the land.

We must identify the deep tension and challenge in which many of us journey. If we don't, then we miss something along the way: we miss truly living life on the land today. We've been taught that we're sinners; we've been taught to repent; we've been taught that through Christ's blood, we're forgiven and that we will go to heaven when we die. All of this is true—and there is so much more. Truly living today is the call of our lives in Christ.

Within these truths, keep in mind these two stories from Jesus' earthly journey. First, Jesus challenged Mary and Martha, when their brother Lazarus lay in the tomb, to see life not only in the truth of eternal life someday, but life that very day in Him. Jesus challenged them to see Him as the resurrection and the life. Jesus called Lazarus forth from the tomb to live (John 11). In the second story, Jesus challenged the woman at the well to see Him as living water from which she could drink for life today. She knew the Messiah was to come. Jesus said, "I who speak to you am He." The woman drank deeply and lived (John 4).

Christ Jesus calls us to trust that He is the life in whom we live for eternity, a future event, which is now in Him. As branches grafted into Christ, we live grafted into our inheritance today and for all eternity. And there is vastly more! Christ lives in us. The new covenant is not tied to a specific land or to God dwelling in the temple, as was the old covenant. It is fulfilled in Christ, and Christ is in us.

We journey on the land as sojourners, as those dwelling in but not fully at home on this land. With eyes on the promised land, face-to-face with Christ for all eternity, we are right here, right now. Growing is necessary for living, and we are called to grow. With proper care, water, food, and light, grapevines grow. Jesus gave us the vine image, as well as declaring Himself living water, the bread of life, and the light of the world, to help us grow and cling to Him while journeying on the land.

As we live in Christ, and He lives in us, we grow—and delight in meditating upon this marvel. God promised and provided the Promised Land. Our earthly journey through a life of faith in Christ leads to the promised land someday—yet it is now. We picture our loved ones in heaven, singing eternal praises to the Lamb on the throne. We join with them when we celebrate the Lord's Supper, feasting and being nourished by Christ's body and blood. God invited the patriarchs to visualize living in the Promised Land, and God invites us to do the same.

Journey there. Visualize heaven as a place of peace and rest. Let your heart see the majesty and beauty of God's promises fulfilled for you. Let your heart rest assured that God has worked His work for you. Rest. Be at peace because the promised land, where there are no more tears, suffering, or death, is yours.

Journey here, too, into the reality that in order to dwell in heaven face-to-face with Christ, we must face dying and death. We must breathe our final breath. We must die to enter our final resting place in heaven. This topic takes courage and strength to address. Why? Acknowledging our mortality is difficult because we were not created to die, but rather to live eternally. Death entered our story because of Adam's disobedience.

All people face death as a result of their punishment. The apostle Paul reflected both on death and on the promise:

> For if, because of one man's trespass, death reigned through that one man, much more will those who receive the abundance of grace and the free gift of righteousness reign in life through the one man Jesus Christ. Therefore, as one trespass led to condemnation for all men, so one act of righteousness leads to justification and life for all men. For as by the one man's disobedience the many were made sinners, so by the one man's obedience the many will be made righteous. Romans 5:17–19

"Be strong and courageous" were God's words to Moses and Moses' words to Joshua and Joshua's words to the children of Israel as they prepared to enter the Promised Land. "Be strong and courageous" are God's words for us. Strength and courage are absolutely critical to addressing dying and death—and for entering the promised land. With heaven assured and in full view, we have the courage to say, "One day I will die." We don't know how or when, but we will die.

The apostle Paul encourages us to believe that we have already died and our lives are hidden with God in Christ (see Colossians 3:1–3). We are that tiny bud, cut away from the old and placed into the True Vine. We live in Christ; He is eternal and we are eternal in Him. We are called to grow, bear fruit, and thrive wherever we dwell and whatever our circumstance. Paul said, "As you received Christ Jesus the Lord, so walk in Him, rooted and built up in Him and established in the faith, just as you were taught, abounding in thanksgiving" (Colossians 2:6–7).

Strength and courage open possibilities for us; strength and courage allow us to confront the hard questions of life. Grafted into the eternal life of Christ, eyes looking up and out, we live and sojourn on the land. During

Father

Son

Holy Spirit

Emotions
Body
Heart
Soul
Mind
Senses
Spirit

the journey of faith and life, positioned IN Christ for all eternity, we say with Paul, "In all these things we are more than conquerors through Him who loved us. For I am sure that neither death nor life, nor angels nor rulers, nor things present nor things to come, nor powers, nor height nor depth, nor anything else in all creation, will be able to separate us from the love of God in Christ Jesus our Lord" (Romans 8:37–39).

Living on the land is unique for every individual. Each individual embraces the journey uniquely too. Here are some of the journey questions I've confronted as I've grown as a branch of the True Vine. At times, strong Christian people have mentored me in my journey, and at other times I've confronted these questions in solitude with Christ as my companion. The desire to run away from or go around tough questions is powerful, but not as powerful as my desire to live. In Christ, with strength and courage, I chose and continue to choose the journey.

- What healthy and helpful aspects of my generational heritage do I embrace for the journey today?

- What painful and unhealthy aspects of my generational heritage do I choose to learn from but not embrace today?

- Does my being define my doing or does my doing define my being? Am I a human being or a human doing?

- Do I give myself permission to think about how I think? Growing and living means journeying into a deeper understanding of how God created and redeemed me to be free.

The call to trust Christ as our rest, both here in this land and for eternity in the promised land, is very real. Christ provides the strength and courage to live as sojourners here as we dwell in His holy, eternal life. Embracing that life breeds honesty, authenticity, and transparency in us and in those around us as we sojourn together. Like the woman at the well, we drink deeply of living water; like Lazarus, we come forth from death to life at Christ's call.

For individual study, meditate on the following questions and additional Scriptures. For small-group study, discuss these thoughts and questions:

1. Chronicle your journey in the land. Write the places or homes in which you've lived, then record experiences in those places, both joy-filled and painful.

2. Visualize Christ as your rest, your dwelling place. Discern where you are now. How is your faith and trust challenged by seeing Christ as your dwelling place? your rest?

3. Write your journey questions; pray for strength and courage.

4. For additional study, read and reflect upon Acts 7. Stephen, just before being killed for proclaiming the Messiah, summarized God's promise to his forefathers as well as the gift of the promised land.

The Upper Yosemite Falls,
Yosemite National Park.

Chapter Ten

THE EARTH

The earth is made of rock in many and varied forms, and so we consider earth as we continue and complete our journey through *The Rock Speaks*. The outer shell of the earth upon which the surface of the earth rests is the continental crust; the ocean floor is called the oceanic crust. The crust of this amazing planet is proportionately thin to its overall size. The oceanic crust is 4 miles thick and the continental crust is more than 30 miles thick. Those surface depths account for between .001 and .004 percent of the earth. There are approximately 3,950 miles to the center of the earth's core.

The layers of the earth, from the inside out, are the inner core, outer core, the lower mantle, and the upper mantle. Over the last five hundred years, modern technology and modern science have facilitated discovery that is beyond my imagination. Discovery continues as science advances and as scientists build on the knowledge accumulated through the generations. When I think of modern advances, I try to imagine my grandmother's perspective of the earth.

Hazel Steinbeck, my father's mother, was born in 1910 and died in 2007 at ninety-seven years of age. Her parents farmed the same land I do, using horses and mules. She remembered their first car and their first phone. She remembered the exciting day when electricity finally came far enough out of Paso Robles for this house to be connected. In 1930, she journeyed to San Francisco by train to work as a nanny for a wealthy family. She was amazed at how many vehicles were in the city!

My grandfather was called away from his young family to serve as a chaplain in World War II, and he shipped out across the vast ocean into the European Theater. I also think of stories Grandma was told about her grandparents' journey to America in the 1860s across that very same ocean. Travelling the earth wasn't easy, but my family did it.

Technology has advanced at breakneck speed since the turn of the century, and especially since 2007. We hop in our cars or on planes in a very mobile society. We turn on the GPS, which tells us exactly where we are and takes us exactly where we want to go. We can hold our small cell phone in our hand, open Google Earth and type in our address, and in crystal-clear 3-D, we can look at our streets and homes. We can view the terrain exactly as it is in our little spaces of this amazing earth. We can look at our high-definition screens and watch the rotation of the earth from space through satellites. We watch the earth rotating and can accept that scientific fact in our brains, yet because of its constant speed and our relative size, our bodies cannot feel the earth's rotation.

Although we cannot feel the earth spinning, we've developed language like "My world is spinning out of control" and "My head is spinning over the news." That language gives us insight. When our equilibrium is healthy, we live a balanced life. Our eyes, brain, and ears contribute to living in balance on this spinning earth. In addition to our bodies keeping us in balance, our complex inner being contributes to balance, or the

lack of it. Our soul, spirit, heart, and emotions play a critical role in living a balanced life.

Balance is relatively easy to maintain when we are young. But as we grow older, when one or more aspects of our being are ignored, balance is difficult to maintain and we may feel like life is spinning out of control. Some call these times a "midlife crisis." I call it a wake-up call to pay attention to all aspects of our complex being. Through the Scriptures and the theme of the earth, we will explore God's wake-up call to the importance of nurturing our whole being.

Gravity teaches this too. We could not exist without the intricate balance of spinning and the gravitational pull toward the center of the earth. We've developed language like "Words cannot express the gravity of this situation," with "gravity" meaning importance, significance, weight, consequence, magnitude. Falling down gives us insight into gravity. When I trip and fall, I fall down, not up. Unless I pull off a very athletic move, I fall with a thud and need to assess the gravity of the situation before popping up again. When my spirit and soul are heavy, the gravity of the moment draws my shoulders, back, and eyes downward.

With imagery of the earth as a springboard into this chapter of *The Rock Speaks*, we embrace our deep desire to grasp more fully God's mercy and grace for us. We lift our eyes and hearts to the wisdom of the Scriptures for insights that will help us grow in faith and understanding and that will help us embrace God's creation of this earth and our life in Christ on this earth.

From Heaven to Earth

God the Son chose to leave the perfection of heaven to dwell in human flesh on the earth He had created. Thousands of years and many promises after Adam and Eve were cast out of the Garden of Eden, our Lord chose life on earth in order to fulfill our Creator's promise of redemption, to live and be perfection for us. He became our perfect home, our abiding place. Christ's perfect life, His mercy through calling, healing, and restoring people to Himself, His suffering, His death, His resurrection, and His ascension satisfied the demands of His Father, the Creator of heaven and earth. Paul declared, "For our sake He made Him to be sin who knew no sin, so that in Him we might become the righteousness of God" (2 Corinthians 5:21).

Near the end of His earthly ministry, Jesus ministered to His disciples in the Upper Room. We are blessed to have John's record of Jesus washing the disciples' feet, calling out Judas as betrayer, declaring Himself the way, the truth, and the life. We have Jesus' words as He declared Himself the vine and His followers the branches (John 15–16). Just before going out to face arrest and crucifixion, Christ prayed:

> Father, the hour has come; glorify Your Son that the Son may glorify You, since You have given Him authority over all flesh, to give eternal life to all whom You have given Him. And this is eternal life, that they know You the only true God, and Jesus Christ whom You have sent. I glorified You on earth, having accomplished the work that You gave Me to do. And now, Father, glorify Me in Your own presence with the glory that I had with You before the world existed. John 17:2–5

Jesus' prayer spoke a confident "amen" to the work of the cross and grave that still lay ahead. This wonderful expression of a future glory through suffering is critical to us as we are called to grow in faith in Christ today, on this earth. We will face suffering in this life, yet we have already died with Christ; we have already risen with Christ. Salvation in Christ will be complete one day; salvation in Christ is complete now. Healing will be complete one day; healing in Christ is complete now.

The South Window, Arches National Park in eastern Utah.

Jesus' words and deeds during His short earthly ministry fulfilled this exact purpose. Imagine the blind beggars of whom Jesus asked, "What do you want Me to do for you?" Jesus fulfilled their simple request, "We want to see." His touch granted sight to the blind in more than one way. Their blind eyes were opened and their cry for mercy was met by the Savior, who opened their hearts to His work. Scripture says, "They . . . followed Him" (see Matthew 20:29–34).

Imagine the lame walking and the deaf hearing and the dead being raised. These events were a glorious fulfillment of the kingdom of heaven in Christ. The word and work of Christ accomplished so much more! The physical healing of the body was one aspect of the word and work of Christ. Drawing people to Himself for eternity, healing their heart, soul, and spirit, was also the reality that accompanied the physical healing.

We are invited to ask God in Christ to heal our physical and emotional suffering. At times He answers our prayers with miraculous healing. At times He works through the hands of ministers, health care professionals, therapists, and counselors. We may not be healed physically or emotionally, which gives us an amazing opportunity to trust that He is at work in our lives in ways much deeper than a visible healing. It also gives us an opportunity to be an example of faith and strength to those around us. At all times, Christ answers our deepest need for full and complete healing now, which will be fully realized when we pass through death and the grave to live face-to-face with Him for eternity.

THY WILL BE DONE ON EARTH

Christ invites us to see with eyes of faith the healing, forgiveness, and mercy that are fully ours in Him even now. Christ also invites us to a life of prayer into an intimate, conversational relationship with Him. He calls us to ask, to pray in His name as His brothers and sisters, and to be confident that He will do what we ask in His name according to His will. He also instructed us how to pray with these words:

> Our Father in heaven, hallowed be Your name. Your kingdom come, Your will be done, on earth as it is in heaven. Give us this day our daily bread, and forgive us our debts, as we also have forgiven our debtors. Matthew 6:9–12

Praying Jesus' words "Your will be done, on earth as it is in heaven" is a really big prayer! We meditate on those words coupled with the surrounding words about God's kingdom coming, as well as forgiving and receiving forgiveness. What is God's will in heaven? What is God's will on earth? What does "Your kingdom come" mean for us? What does it mean to be forgiven by God and to forgive those who have wronged us?

Our understanding of these important words and questions cannot possibly encompass the whole of Jesus' heart as He instructed His followers to pray this way. We humbly sit at Jesus' feet and allow our discussion and study to be guided by His life and ministry and words as He walked this earth. We ask God to guide our hearts so that we can comprehend and accept the rich meaning of Jesus' words and work as He fulfilled the prayer He taught us to pray.

Jesus' first proclamation in Matthew's Gospel was "Repent, for the kingdom of heaven is at hand." He spoke these words after His Baptism in the Jordan River and after His forty-day journey in the desert, where He prayed, fasted, and confronted Satan's lies and temptation. "Your kingdom come" is fulfilled in Christ. Paraphrased, it says, "The kingdom of God is here because I am here in your midst."

Jesus' entire life and ministry were the fulfillment of the kingdom of God on earth. His words and His work accomplished "Thy kingdom

Mount Olympus, located in Olympic National Park, is the highest peak in the western Washington mountain range.

come on earth as it is in heaven." His word and work for us and in us and through us continues. Said differently, Jesus accomplished His father's will then *and* continues now in an ongoing fulfillment that is complete.

Jesus' words on the cross, "It is finished," help us dig deeper into the fulfillment of the will of God on earth as it is in heaven and the continuation of that completed work. ALL aspects of the Commandments were fulfilled in the life of Christ, as He did not come to abolish the laws and commands, but to fulfill them (Matthew 5:17). Christ's cry from the cross, "It is finished," meant that He had met God's perfect demand for an unblemished sacrifice. Our righteousness cannot meet the highest standard required for entering the kingdom of heaven. Christ's "It is finished" brought the kingdom of God to us then, which was accomplished and continues to be accomplished in us now.

The will of God being done on earth as it is in heaven is not our doing. We are receivers, human beings as opposed to human doings, according to the will of God. We are passive; He is active. He is Creator of the heavens and the earth; God the Son is the Re-Creator of the relationship between us and God the Father. Having received, we are "doers" of the will of God as we do the work God places in front of us. His workmanship, His masterpiece. We are Christ's hands, feet, and voice in this world. Paul said:

> For by grace you have been saved through faith. And this is not your own doing; it is the gift of God, not a result of works, so that no one may boast. For we are His workmanship, created in Christ Jesus for good works, which God prepared beforehand, that we should walk in them. Ephesians 2:8–10

Jesus' instruction to pray "Give us this day our daily bread" opens our hearts to see the earth as the place through which He provides food to fulfill this petition. Farmers are the doers through whom God works to provide the answer to this prayer. In our modern world, there are a plethora of stages that must be fulfilled in order to bring food to our grocery stores. God works through farmers, technology, truckers, and all of the hands that place the food on the shelves.

We also have an opportunity to worship Christ as the bread of life and the living water through God's will being done as He sustains our lives on this earth. The bigger picture includes a faith life that embraces the Word of God as our "daily bread," the Word that sustains our soul, our spirit, our heart, and our mind. The Word of God is the only food that truly satisfies and endures to eternal life. Christ is the living water, the only water that truly satisfies. Trusting this allows us to challenge our way of thinking about food and drink, about eating and drinking, to grow.

God calls us to feed our inner being on Him. He calls us to feed our body with the food and drink we need for physical life. Overeating or undereating to satisfy our hunger is a tremendous physical challenge as well as an emotional and spiritual problem. Drinking the wrong drink to satisfy our thirst is also a spiritual concern. Jesus addresses these in this petition of the Lord's Prayer, "Give us this day our daily bread." Christ's mercy and healing are for us as His will is fulfilled in us as we care for our being.

Jesus instructs us to pray "Forgive us our debts, as we also have forgiven our debtors" under the all-encompassing "Our Father in heaven, hallowed be Your name. Your kingdom come, Your will be done on earth as it is in heaven." God's name is glorified, His kingdom comes, and His will is done on earth when we live forgiveness every moment of every day. Forgiveness and living fully alive are intimately connected. Forgiveness from God is a gift that is grounded in His mercy and love for us, here and in heaven. The forgiveness Jesus won through His blood and sealed by His resurrection fulfilled God's demand for a perfect sacrifice, once and for all. It is finished, and forgiveness continues. Christ's perfect sacrifice and forgiveness free us from condemnation. Christ's perfect sacrifice and forgiveness free us from sin, from guilt, and from shame. By Christ's love and mercy, we are free, clean, whole, healed, and eternal while living now on this earth.

Christ's earthly journey led Him to the bed of a paralyzed man. In the presence of religious leaders who weren't interested in allowing Him authority to speak as God, Jesus said to the man, "Your sins are forgiven." The religious leaders called it blasphemy; followers of Christ called it amazing and extraordinary. Healing that comes through forgiveness in Christ was higher than the physical healing, which Jesus also offered. Jesus' forgiveness and restoration were present always, in all of His words and actions:

> When Jesus perceived their thoughts, He answered them, "Why do you question in your hearts? Which is easier, to say, 'Your sins are forgiven you,' or to say, 'Rise and walk'? But that you may know that the Son of Man has authority on earth to forgive sins"—He said to the man who was paralyzed—"I say to you, rise, pick up your bed and go home." And immediately he rose up before them and picked up what he had been lying on and went home, glorifying God. And amazement seized them all, and they glorified God and were filled with awe, saying, "We have seen extraordinary things today." Luke 5:22–26

The kingdom of God was manifested through Jesus to the people. Our relationship with Him as branches of the one true vine takes place through His work of grafting us into His life. The image of grafting is one way to picture Baptism into Christ's life. Forgiveness from God means growing and aliveness in a flesh-on-flesh relationship. Healing and oxygen, life and breath, come through Christ's blood, regardless of the physical condition of our earthly bodies.

Believing Christ's forgiveness in the depth of our being, with our heart and not simply with our brain, is challenging! Believing that Christ's forgiveness is "for *me*," not just "for you," leads us to ask challenging questions like those listed at the end of the previous chapter. Do I believe, as Peter said, that by His wounds I have been healed (1 Peter 2:24)? Do I believe that forgiveness means growing and aliveness even when my body and mind are failing? Can I receive Christ at His Word, receive His forgiveness for me? God has freed us! Please ask, "Have I freed myself from the inner conflicts and negative self-talk? What work is God working here and now in me?"

Receiving forgiveness from God frees us to live in relationship with one another on this earth. Having been freed, we can free others who have wounded us. This is where the rubber hits the road in our Christian faith. Whether we are among our families, at home, at church, or at work, we have plenty of opportunities to practice what we believe. We cherish courage, authenticity, and honesty. Here are a few examples:

1. When I've hurt someone, I go to him or her and genuinely say, "I'm sorry, please forgive me." We give that person opportunity to free us. Relationship is restored through forgiveness. At times, if the hurt is big, they may have a very difficult time forgiving me. If that is the case, I must humbly live with that and pray that the relationship would someday be restored.

2. When someone has hurt me, he or she may come to me and ask for forgiveness. My heart may struggle to say "I forgive you." Having been forgiven by God, we have opportunity to live the forgiveness we've been given. Grudges and payback have no place in hearts of love and mercy. Relationships are restored through forgiveness.

3. When someone has hurt me, he or she may not come to me and ask for forgiveness. Going to that person to say that he or she has hurt me may be necessary. That person may or may not respond to my words. Scripture instructs us to take others with us in an attempt to restore the relationship so that we can live in harmony (see Matthew 18).

4. Abusive relationships require great caution when it comes to forgiveness. A victim may have an opportunity, if the environment is safe, to express forgiveness to an abuser face-to-face. However, a victim may never have an opportunity to forgive an attacker face-to-face. An attacker may never have an opportunity to ask for forgiveness face-to-face. Forgiveness in the heart of the victim is truly possible and frees the victim of the abuser's power. In many cases, hearts are freed, but relationships must not be restored.[10]

5. Living fully in the forgiveness of sins also means that we allow God's forgiveness to permeate our entire being. We grow and learn to live, forgiving ourselves as God has forgiven us. While a simple statement, truly receiving God's forgiveness and being merciful with ourselves in our daily lives isn't so simple.

These examples show the complex nature of living in relationship with one another, in forgiveness with one another. Christ walked this earth to restore relationships, and He continues to be God with us, giving us courage to live as His holy people. Our biggest hurts come through relationships; healing comes through relationships too. One of the greatest temptations we face is receiving forgiveness from God but not living forgiveness toward our neighbor.

Christ spoke the following very challenging words immediately after the Lord's Prayer in Matthew's Gospel: "For if you forgive others their

---

10 Many resources are available to victims of abuse, which should be used by the victims themselves and by their families. The Lutheran Church—Missouri Synod commissioned a domestic violence task force whose information can be accessed here: *www.lcms.org/socialissues/domesticviolence*

trespasses, your heavenly Father will also forgive you, but if you do not forgive others their trespasses, neither will your Father forgive your trespasses" (Matthew 6:14–15). Living outside of God's will is a serious matter of the heart. We look in awe at Christ as He hung on the cross and cried out, "Father, forgive them, for they know not what they do" (Luke 23:34).

Christ's actions and healing words on the cross are beyond our human comprehension or ability to imitate, as is every aspect of the call to faith. Christ's call to forgive is grounded in His Word and work, which is extraordinary. He provides everything He demands through His holy life. His is a daily call to live the mercy we've received in our homes, our churches, and our workplaces, in our communities and world. Growing in faith and love and mercy takes place when we receive, take to heart, and act according to the Word of God.

Christ's word and work as He walked the earth included speaking truth into lies and hatred, opening eyes and hearts, healing the sick, and raising the dead. Christ's word and work continue today in us as He calls us to grow in faith and love during our earthly journey. Forgiveness is one aspect of our faith life. Another aspect is allowing Christ into our deep brokenness in order to bring healing. Christ grants us courage to step away from unhealthy relationships and into health and wholeness. Christ calls us to a deep prayer life and desire for intimacy with Him here on earth.

The apostle Paul gives us insight into the will of God on earth: "See that no one repays anyone evil for evil, but always seek to do good to one another and to everyone. Rejoice always, pray without ceasing, give thanks in all circumstances; for this is the will of God in Christ Jesus for you" (1 Thessalonians 5:15–18). Note that Paul says, "give thanks *in* all circumstances," *not* "give thanks *for* all circumstances"! God works through our challenges, pain, and suffering just as He worked through the cross and the grave. We beg God that His will be done in our lives as it is on earth and in heaven.

TEMPORARILY ON THIS EARTH; FOREVER IN HEAVEN

The temporary nature of our lives is a wake-up call to the fact that the earth is also temporary. This earth will pass away, but the Word of God will never pass away (Luke 21:33). Being truly alive, living the journey to which we are called, includes embracing the eternal life of Christ who glorified God on this earth by a perfect life, death, and resurrection. We know that through Christ, our resurrection is the end of the story. Resurrection living is both the end of the story and the now of our stories. Living now means that we have already passed through death into life. Living now means seeing with eyes of faith, in the midst of crosses we bear, the resurrection and the life for us now. Living now means seeing with eyes of faith in the midst of the challenges we face living on this earth, life complete for us and in us. The apostle Paul said:

> If then you have been raised with Christ, seek the things that are above, where Christ is, seated at the right hand of God. Set your minds on things that are above, not on things that are on earth. For you have died, and your life is hidden with Christ in God. When Christ who is your life appears, then you also will appear with Him in glory. Colossians 3:1–4

We set our minds on the things of God because our lives are hidden with Christ in God. We will pass through our final breath and through the grave into eternity. Faith says "amen" to the truth that this future event, "we have died," has already taken place in Christ now. We are baptized into His eternal life; He dwells in us. We set our minds on these eternal truths and truly live today where God has placed us. We are given opportunity after opportunity to grow in Christ and to face challenging journey questions with strength and courage. We are called to live the resurrection now.

THE EARTH QUAKES

The temporary nature of our lives and this earth is very apparent when the earth quakes. I live just a few miles from the San Andreas Fault, so earthquakes have always been a part of my life. Earthquakes come with no warning. Most earthquakes I've experienced feel like the earth rolling under my feet. One earthquake came with a huge boom and the earth moving back and forth. Some people are so terrified of earthquakes that they will never travel to California. I admit, I don't mind feeling earthquakes.

Earthquakes teach us about Christ's creative work. Matthew recorded two earthquakes in his Gospel. They provide an amazing testimony of Christ's completed work on this earth:

> And Jesus cried out again with a loud voice and yielded up His spirit. And behold, the curtain of the temple was torn in two, from top to bottom. And the earth shook, and the rocks were split. The tombs also were opened. And many bodies of the saints who had fallen asleep were raised, and coming out of the tombs after His resurrection they went into the holy city and appeared to many. When the centurion and those who were with him, keeping watch over Jesus, saw the earthquake and what took place, they were filled with awe and said, "Truly this was the Son of God!" Matthew 27:50–54

This first earthquake took place at Jesus' death. He died, the earth quaked, rocks split, dead people came out of their tombs. Imagine the sight! Jesus, Creator, Redeemer, died. People who had died and had been resting in their tombs came forth. Awe led to the exclamation "This was the Son of God!" This is our faith. We will rest in a tomb; we will rise and step forth into life. This belief gives us courage to live life today. The magnitude of this earthquake cannot be measured. We are the beneficiaries of the earthquake that announced the completion of Christ's earthly work, which continues for us and in us today.

The perfect Son of God, the Lamb of God, was sacrificed as an offering on Golgotha's holy hill. Alone to die, Christ cried out, "It is finished!" At the death of the Son of God, the curtain of the temple, which had separated the people from the holiest of holy things of God, was torn in two. The barrier was gone. Christ's life is the holiest of holies, and He grafted us into His holy life. God chose to no longer dwell in the temple. God the Father chose and continues to choose to dwell in the life of His Son—God in Christ and Christ in God and Christ in us. John recorded Jesus' words declaring Himself as the way to God, His Father:

> Philip said to Him, "Lord, show us the Father, and it is enough for us." Jesus said to him, "Have I been with you so long, and you still do not know Me, Philip? Whoever has seen Me has seen the Father. How can you say, 'Show us the Father'? Do you not believe that I am in the Father and the Father is in Me? The words that I say to you I do not speak on My own authority, but the Father who dwells in Me does His works. Believe Me that I am in the Father and the Father is in Me, or else believe on account of the works themselves." John 14:8–11

The resurrection of Christ also involved "a great earthquake." Imagine the two Marys going to the tomb at dawn to finish the burial process. Their hearts were heavy with the gravity of the crucifixion and death of their dear friend just days earlier. The earth shook when the angel of the Lord descended from heaven and rolled back the stone. The guards became like dead men. The angel sat on the stone and declared to Mary and Mary, "Do not be afraid."

> Now after the Sabbath, toward the dawn of the first day of the week, Mary Magdalene and the other Mary went to see the tomb. And behold, there was a great earthquake, for an angel of the Lord descended from heaven and came and rolled back the stone and sat on it. His appearance was like lightning, and his clothing white as snow. And for fear of him the guards trembled and became like dead men. But the angel said to the women, "Do not be afraid, for I know that you seek Jesus who was crucified. He is not here, for He has risen, as He said. Come, see the place where He lay." Matthew 28:1–6

The angel didn't say, "Do not be afraid of the earthquake." The angel said, "Do not be afraid, for I know that you seek Jesus who was crucified. He is not here, for He has risen, as He said. Come, see the place where He lay." Moments later, the risen Lord appeared to the women; His words to them were "Do not be afraid."

The Word of God, paraphrased, says, "Do not be afraid of the things of this earth; they are temporary." Jesus had foretold His death and resurrection, just as the prophets had. The women were witnesses, and we are witnesses to the word and work of Christ. The Word of God says, "Jesus is alive, Jesus is for us, Jesus lives in us eternally, now."

God's will was done on earth through the life, death, and resurrection of His holy Son. God's will on earth is being done through our lives, through our daily death to the things of this world, and through our daily resurrection into life. This daily exercise of faith is earthly practice of the things of heaven; the daily exercise of dying and rising is practice for the day we breathe our last breath and enter into face-to-face eternity with Christ.

The Earth in the Psalms: Meditations

The Psalms, written by those whose faith was in the Messiah, provide rich words upon which to meditate as we conclude our journey through the earth as *The Rock Speaks*.

- O Lord, our Lord, how majestic is Your name in all the earth! Psalm 8:1

- The earth is the Lord's and the fullness thereof, the world and those who dwell therein, for He has founded it upon the seas and established it upon the rivers. Psalm 24:1–2

- For the word of the Lord is upright, and all His work is done in faithfulness. He loves righteousness and justice; the earth is full of the steadfast love of the Lord. By the word of the Lord the heavens were made, and by the breath of His mouth all their host. He gathers the waters of the sea as a heap; He puts the deeps in storehouses. Let all the earth fear the Lord; let all the inhabitants of the world stand in awe of Him! For He spoke, and it came to be; He commanded, and it stood firm. Psalm 33:4–9

- God is our refuge and strength, a very present help in trouble. Therefore we will not fear though the earth gives way, though the mountains be moved into the heart of the sea, though its waters roar and foam, though the mountains tremble at its swelling. . . . Come, behold the works of the Lord, how He has brought desolations on the earth. He makes wars cease to the end of the earth; He breaks the bow and shatters the spear; He burns the chariots with fire. "Be still, and know that I am God. I will be exalted among the nations, I will be exalted in the earth!" The Lord of hosts is with us; the God of Jacob is our fortress. Psalm 46:1–3, 8–11

- As Your name, O God, so Your praise reaches to the ends of the earth. Your right hand is filled with righteousness. Psalm 48:10

- Hear my cry, O God, listen to my prayer; from the end of the earth I call to You when my heart is faint. Lead me to the rock that is higher than I, for You have been my refuge, a strong tower against the enemy. Psalm 61:1–3

- Lord, You have been our dwelling place in all generations. Before the mountains were brought forth, or ever You had formed the earth and the world, from everlasting to everlasting You are God. Psalm 90:1–2

- I lift up my eyes to the hills. From where does my help come? My help comes from the LORD, who made heaven and earth. He will not let your foot be moved; He who keeps you will not slumber. Behold, He who keeps Israel will neither slumber nor sleep. The LORD is your keeper; the LORD is your shade on your right hand. The sun shall not strike you by day, nor the moon by night. The LORD will keep you from all evil; He will keep your life. The LORD will keep your going out and your coming in from this time forth and forevermore. Psalm 121

For individual study, meditate on the following questions. For small-group study, discuss these thoughts and questions:

1. How is God calling you to grow through your deeper understanding of His work on this earth for you?

2. We pray the Lord's Prayer so regularly. Take time to meditate on the words "Your will be done on earth as it is in heaven." How is God's will being done for you today? How is God's will being done through you today?

3. Which of the psalms above touches your inner being and gives you strength and courage? How does it call you to grow in faith and embrace your journey in Christ on this earth?

" The Rock that followed them was Christ" were Paul's words to the people of the city of Corinth, people who needed encouragement for their daily journey of faith. Those words have guided us through our journey into *The Rock Speaks*. Christ among the people, then, is the same Christ, present among us now. The rock imagery provided the road upon which we traveled deep into our hearts and faith.

The humbling experience of writing *The Rock Speaks* was a journey that led me to deeper faith and trust in the Word and work of the triune God through His creation. I am grateful that through my childhood passion for collecting rocks and playing in the dirt, God led me home to the soil and to this vocation. I am grateful that you have chosen to journey with me through *The Rock Speaks*, to more fully grasp God's mercy and love.

The Rock Speaks, I hope and pray, is a stepping-stone to a deeper search of the Scriptures. Continue to look around at the many forms of rock. Observe. Dig into the Scriptures more. Reflect. Grow. Heal. God is

continually at work through His Word to call us closer to Him, to live, to be alive. Allow His Word to work in the soil of your heart.

Planting and tending my garden is a joyous task. Try as I might, however, I cannot garden without getting dirty, without a mess. God's work through Christ's life, death, and resurrection was messy. God's work in our hearts is messy too. Life is messy, and death is messy. Try as we might, we cannot live without messes. God's work is not neat and tidy because He doesn't stay at a distance. He dwells in us and works His work in us. God calls us to know ourselves and to continue growing in faith toward Him, in understanding of ourselves, and in love for our neighbor.

The ongoing blessing and challenge in life is to more fully grasp the faith that God, our rock and our strength, works through our messes and beauty, providing bountiful opportunities for growth, faith, and trust in Him. Prayerfully, through the Word of God, through dust and sand, rock and soil, hills and mountains, you have come to a greater understanding of our Lord's creative work today for you and in you and through you.

More from Cindy Steinbeck!

The Vine Speaks: Eleven Lessons from John 15 uses imagery and metaphor of the vineyard to explore how Christ works in us. Lessons are drawn from the vineyard, the lives of the apostles, the author's experiences, and from our own circumstances and perspectives.

For more information about this Bible study, go to www.cph.org.
Item 204164.

Eleven Lessons from John 15

The Vine Speaks

CINDY STEINBECK

The Vine Speaks!

Vines cannot talk, but vines speak. Three hundred thousand grapevines in our family's vineyard have spoken to me. I am at home on the soil, among the vines. My faith has grown by watching our vines grow. My faith and understanding of it have grown by watching the work my father does and by observing the work our employees accomplish. And I've grown by working on and among the vines.

I am continuously learning what it means to be at home and to grow as a branch in The Vine—Christ Jesus. Here in the pages of *The Vine Speaks*, I share some of the truths I've discovered among the grapevines and some of the details of my journey in the life of The Vine. For me, being at home and growing in Christ, The Vine, means welcoming growth in my heart, mind, and life. Growth is not easy because it usually means change, and change is hard—but growth is the way of life in The Vine. I invite you to see through my eyes what Jesus may have meant in John 15:5 when He declared Himself "the vine" and us "the branches."

The Vine Speaks is a conversational Bible study springing from Jesus' words "I am the vine; you are the branches." Each chapter begins with the heading "The Vine Speaks: My Father's Vineyard." In this section, I offer my understanding of grapevines and the vineyard as it relates to this Bible passage. I did not study viticulture in college, but I've worked among the vines long enough to pick up on vineyard practices. Please imagine a tour with me through my vineyard and process with me my observations. Smell the soil, watch the growth, taste the fruit, and observe the seasonal changes.

Chapter One

THE VINE

THE VINE SPEAKS: MY FATHER'S VINEYARD

Agrapevine speaks, but it cannot talk. The vines speak to me as I live and work in my father's vineyard in Paso Robles, California. (I own the vineyard, too, but to me it sounds better when I call it "my father's vineyard.")

In 1997, the vines called me home from a professional ministry career as a director of Christian education. The Vine, Christ Jesus, calls each of us to be at home in Him today in a rich, alive, growing sense. My hope is that this magnificent plant God created, the grapevine, will speak to you as it does to me. I pray that God will work through my understanding of the vine so that The Vine speaks to you as you read this book.

Vineyard practices vary, but there are some basic, common practices that provide the springboard for our study:

- Grapevines need soil in which to be planted, water, and nutrients.

- Grapevines need to be trained, pruned, and thinned. There are challenges a grower of vines faces, and if a vine isn't growing, there are problems that need to be addressed.

- Grapevines have a basic structure, including the root system, which is entirely underground.
- They have a trunk that was once a supple branch and has been trained up and remains for the life of the vine.
- Vines in a vineyard have a graft union into which the varietal was grafted.
- Vines contain branches, tendrils, leaves, buds, and fruit.
- The goal of growing grapevines is fruit production, which in my family's business is crafted into premium dry wine.

The following sketched diagrams help define terms associated with growing grapes and give a foundation for Jesus' words "I am the vine; you are the branches." This is not a technical manual on the physiology of the grapevine; it is a work about the heart of Jesus, The Vine, and His call to grow in Him from the context of the vine.

Grapevines are stunningly beautiful, but it seems to me that everyone who comes to our vineyard for wine tasting is drawn to the vine on a far deeper level than its exterior beauty. Guests love our dusty, bumpy vineyard Jeep tour. They love hearing about the work going on in the field at any given time, and they are fascinated that grapevines need so much care and so many hands-on touches in order to produce premium fruit. After an in-depth look at the vine, guests at my father's vineyard have a far greater appreciation for a glass of wine.

Grapevines grow and bear fruit for thirty to fifty years. Every year in the life of the vine is intimately connected to previous and future years. A microscopic look at a cross section of a bud prior to bud break reveals this wonder. All of the coming year's growth, including the leaves and fruit, is tightly wound up inside the bud. Tiny buds grew on a shoot last year,

Pruned Vine

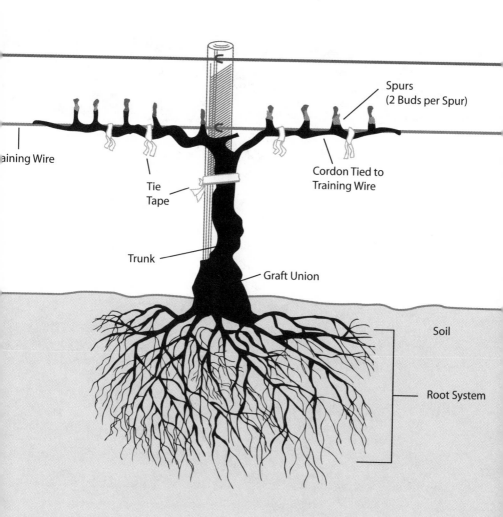

Spurs
(2 Buds per Spur)

Training Wire

Cordon Tied to
Training Wire

Tie
Tape

Trunk

Graft Union

Soil

Root System

Mature Vine

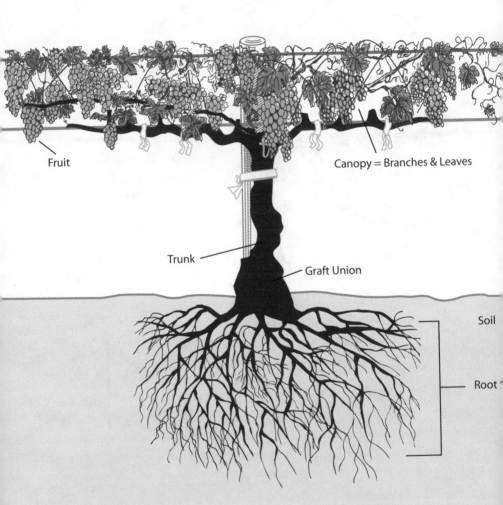

Fruit

Canopy = Branches & Leaves

Trunk

Graft Union

Soil

Root

which was grown on wood from the previous year. Every year in the life of the vine is connected to the past and to the future.

Another foundational principle of growing vines—or any other type of farming, for that matter—is sustainability. The soil and other natural resources are magnificent gifts from our Creator. God provides, and we use the gifts wisely. We love the land, and we take great care to sustain it. We know that it provides our livelihood and our lifestyle. Every decision we make takes into account safety for our families, workers, and the community; every action must be economically sustainable so the next generations can also live off the land.

These two examples—of the present bud connected to both the past and the future and of the soil, which must be sustained—provide rich analogies for our study. Take the first example deeper: the present moment in our lives is intimately connected to our past as well as to our future. God's Word calls us to live fully and grow continually in the present while honoring our past and anticipating His work for our future. He calls us to trust that His work in our lives brings forth growth and fruit.

The second example leads us to confess that life is truly sustainable only in and through Christ, The Vine. Sustainability means stewardship of the gifts we've been given—the soil and natural resources, the environment, and the future of our land and families. In the richest sense of the word, sustainability in The Vine means living and dwelling in Christ in the present and for eternity. Life is truly sustainable in The Vine.

THE VINEDRESSER SPEAKS:
GOD'S WORD FROM THE OLD TESTAMENT

Every moment of God's work is intimately connected to His past work and to His future work. Jesus said, "I am the true vine and My Father is the vinedresser." A vinedresser is a master gardener, one who oversees the vines and makes decisions for the health and growth of a vine. A later chapter is devoted to The Vinedresser. But for now, ponder these words of introduction from the Old Testament, The Vinedresser's words about a vine. (As you do, note that the vine speaking is not a new concept!) These verses are a fascinating account of God speaking in parable form to get the children of Israel to wake up to the evil that Abimelech had committed against his family and Israel. Olive trees and a grapevine shared this conversation about the crowning of the new, evil king:

> And the trees said to the vine, "You come and reign over us." But *the vine said to them,* "Shall I leave my wine that cheers God and men and go hold sway over the trees?" Then all the trees said to the bramble, "You come and reign over us." And the bramble said to the trees, "If in good faith you are anointing me king over you, then come and take refuge in my shade, but if not, let fire come out of the bramble and devour the cedars of Lebanon." (Judges 9:12–15, emphasis added)

The imagery of the vine was spoken by almost every author of the Old Testament. Through the prophets, God spoke punishment through the vine. One form of punishment He rained down on the people was that they would plant a vineyard but not enjoy the fruit or the wine from it. Ouch! That was serious punishment.

God also promised deliverance using vineyard imagery. The Vinedresser said, "They shall plant vineyards and eat their fruit" (Isaiah 65:21). And a beautiful promise using the vine imagery comes through the psalmist's words as he declared that God brought a vine out of Egypt and planted it:

> You brought a *vine out of Egypt;* You drove out the nations and planted it. You cleared the ground for it; *it took deep root and filled the land.* The mountains were covered with its shade, the mighty cedars with its branches. It sent out its branches to the sea and its shoots to the River. Why then have You broken down its walls, so that all who pass along the way pluck its fruit? The boar from the forest ravages it, and all that move in the field feed on it.

> Turn again, O God of hosts! Look down from heaven, and see; *have regard for this vine, the stock that Your right hand planted, and for the son whom You made strong for Yourself.* They have burned it with fire; they have cut it down; may they perish at the rebuke of Your face! But let Your hand be on the man of Your right hand, the son of man whom You have made strong for Yourself! Then we shall not turn back from You; give us life, and we will call upon Your name!

> Restore us, O LORD God of hosts! Let Your face shine, that we may be saved! (Psalm 80:8–19, emphasis added)

Jesus is The Vine that God brought up out of Egypt. He was planted. He was ravaged. God had regard for the stock He planted with His right hand and made His Son strong for His purpose—life and salvation in and through The Vine. The Vinedresser desires that we know His heart and grow according to the work of His hands. The Vine speaks to us today, calling us to allow The Vinedresser's work, which is to grow and bear mature fruit in Him.

THE VINE SPEAKS: JESUS' WORDS

I am the true vine, and My Father is the vinedresser. Every branch in Me that does not bear fruit He takes away, and every branch that does bear fruit He prunes, that it may bear more fruit. Already you are clean because of the word that I have spoken to you. Abide in Me, and I in you. As the branch cannot bear fruit by itself, unless it abides in the vine, neither can you, unless you abide in Me. I am the vine; you are the branches. Whoever abides in Me and I in him, he it is that bears much fruit, for apart from Me you can do nothing. (John 15:1–5)

Jesus' words "I am the vine" would have resonated with those of Jewish heritage, who had heard the punishments and promises using vine imagery. What may have been new to them was Jesus' declaration that God was The Vinedresser! That was a job only for poor peasants (more in chapter 5). Jesus spoke the words "I am the vine" just before He left the Upper Room to face the cross. These words are the context from which He calls His followers to abide in Him, to keep His commands, to ask anything in His name, and to bear fruit that will last.